A GREATER VISION
Back from Abortion

By Joan Ulicny

Queenship

PUBLISHING COMPANY
P.O. Box 220 • Goleta, CA 93116
(800) 647-9882 • (805) 692-0043 • Fax: (805) 967-5843

DEDICATION

To my eternal Mother who has bestowed upon me the grace of a greater vision.

Cover Design: Dominic Leo

© 1995 Queenship Publishing

Library of Congress Number: 95-69787

ISBN: 1-882972-44-9

Published by:
Queenship Publishing
P.O. Box 220
Goleta, CA 93116
(800) 647-9882 • (805) 692-0043 • Fax: (805) 967-5843

Printed in the United States of America

ACKNOWLEDGMENTS

I HAVE BEEN BLESSED with many special individuals in my life who had provided me the encouragement and support I needed to persist in this writing, and I struggle with the fear of overlooking anyone, who, in some way, contributed to my completion of this writing. I can only hope that anyone who should be acknowledged here but is not will be acknowledged by the Mother who inspired "A Greater Vision," for, Her thanks would be far greater than any I could offer. Still, there are those, firmly imprinted upon my heart, and upon my life, without whom this work could never have been realized.

First, and foremost, to my parents, Rita and Joseph Ulicny, who taught me more about parenthood and unconditional love in the five years I returned to live with them than I could have learned in a lifetime. True love cannot really be proven until tested, and their patient endurance of all that was burdened them after the accident only increased my love and respect for these two people God had chosen to bring me into the world. To my sister, Jean, whose love for me sustained me when I was far too injured to love myself. I am so in awe of the strength and courage you showed me when I could not find the same within myself. Thank you, Jeanie, for your unceasing desire to remind me during the initial years of my recovery that I was, in your eyes, much more than what the accident had reduced me to. You have taught me much about pain, and made me question whose pain is the greater, the one who does the actual suffering, or those on the sidelines observing the suffering of the loved one. We both know the answer, now....don't we?

To the God-sent instruments in my life, none of whom I would ever have come to know had the accident not occurred. To all the personnel at Pittsburgh's Allegheny General Hospital who fought to keep me alive, particularly Dr. Daniel Diamond. To the special messengers of my Blessed Mother who provided the example of Christian love I needed to instruct me along my journey in faith: Sister Agnes McCormick, Father Don Reinfredt, Father Vincent Cvictovic, and especially, Father John McFadden, who taught me more about what it means to serve God than any other person I have ever known. Father John, you will never know the gift you have been to me or how very much you are loved.

Finally, to my editor and friend, Sherry K. Brennan, who worked so diligently to help bring this work to the exactitude inspired by the Mother who chose her for this purpose. As our respect for one another has grown in the two years we worked together on this manuscript, so, too, has the awe of how God works His will in the lives of those He chooses for His purpose.

CONTENTS

FOREWORD

STORIES OF AN INDIVIDUAL'S RELATIONSHIP with God or one's experiences in faith are rarely found on bestseller lists. These stories seem to be dismissed by the general public who cast such stories as readings for only those with a heightened awareness of their own spirituality, or, for people who truly need such stories to help carry them through some crisis in their lives. These opinions describe a modern world which places its hope and trust in science and technology for answers to the endless challenges facing the world today.

God is usually the last to be called upon when seeking answers to the numerous difficulties and confusions found in the world today. And yet it is impossible to find answers or at least some understanding men and women seek today, without the help of God.

I understand this turn to science and technology for answers that are prompted by illness, disease and handicaps, and a sense of loss. I understand because I pursued these very sources in my search for a cure, a restoration of the physical health I had lost as a result of a horrific accident. I, too, sought out answers from a world that could not give me the answers I wanted to hear. Only when I had exhausted all my efforts in finding the cure to my affliction through science and technology, only then did I approach God. Unlike the rest, He embraced me and gave me the love and help the world could not.

God's response to my call to Him was not the instant physical cure I had expected. He wanted to reveal to me and to teach me the possibilities of a relationship with Him, a relationship that necessarily had to be refined over and over again, until I realized that God truly desired for me to come to know Him more intimately than I had ever thought possible. True intimacy with my God was made possible through my acceptance of my cross—together we shared my suffering, a suffering I could have never endured alone, and this sharing binds me to Him forever.

My learning came from my suffering, and the prompter, the preparer for these teachings was my heavenly Mother. She patiently assisted me as I traveled on my own private road to Calvary, never leaving my side, regardless of my many protests that I needed neither Her nor Her Son. During particular times of despair and self-pity, She drew ever nearer to me and provided me with hope and the courage to continue. My own doubts were somehow transformed through Her Hands into perseverance and patient endurance.

As my awareness of Her presence and role in my life increased, I grew in awe of this Mother of mine to whom nothing seemed impossible, especially the conversion of this particular daughter. She became my solace, and I came to cling to Her when I felt as if I were drowning in an ocean of depression and fear that so often threatened to carry me away from Her, and from the God I had lost once before. There would be no losing Him, this time.

My Blessed Mother would become my teacher, my companion in suffering, my support in a world where human relationships often seemed fleeting, or, perhaps, too judgmental.

When my Blessed Mother re-entered my life after the accident, She would caress my open wounds until they were brought to full healing under Her gentle touch. Before I could learn about healing, however, I first had to learn about suffering—my Mother of Wisdom would teach me. She would teach me to endure my suffering, and from this, gain compassion for myself and others. Until I learned about suffering through my own suffering, I could never identify with the suffering of Her Son, or the suffering of anyone else. She held out the hope only Her Son could provide me, that I might hold out that same hope to others in a world so desperately in search of hope. I believe this is why my Mother came to me—this is why She comes, now, in so many places, to show us the hope that only God can give.

She has been my inspiration, my guide, and the provider of my greater vision.

INTRODUCTION

ON JUNE 7, 1988, I BEGAN WRITING my story, something I had felt compelled to do for many months. As of that date, it had been exactly 19 months and five days since the accident that almost took my life. The seed of this writing was planted on the day of the accident. I was 29 years old. Overwhelmed by my injuries and the realization that something so horrible could actually happen to me, I was paralyzed with a fear greater than any I had ever known.

As my fear grew, and as I realized that it could totally incapacitate me, I began to fight back. I fought to regain the life I had once known and cherished, a life I had worked diligently to attain, a life that was unjustly taken from me. Yet, deep within me, I knew that my life would never be the same; that I would never be the same, and I mourned that loss for many, many months, refusing to accept the reality that was, indeed, mine.

I was consumed with fear, and yet I was provided with enough strength and courage to fight back, a strength and courage, I recognize now, which was not borne of myself; instead it was a gift from My Creator. When I so desperately cried out for something to hold on to in my despair, He heard my cries, saw my fear, and, in time, He answered me. The first lesson I had to learn was patience; that all comes in God's time, not mine — a difficult lesson for a young woman who thought she controlled so much.

Could I do it? Could I start all over again? Was I strong enough to even try? How I struggled with the thought of rebuilding my life. The task before me seemed insurmountable, and I felt so broken, so incapable. I knew that starting my life over again was one project I could not under-take alone. "How does one do that?" I asked myself, "Where do I begin in this process of rebuilding?" I knew that many people were forced into this same position, and I knew that more than a few had succeeded in rebuilding their lives. "God bless them," I thought, full of self pity. I was not "many people," and I harbored no grand illusions of making a comeback with any notoriety. I was, simply, bitter.

I was a young woman who had worked diligently for all she had attained, and I made no excuses to anyone for my success. I had adopted an attitude, perhaps too preva-lent among young people in the eighties, that I was some-how entitled to all I had achieved and attained. What's wrong with that? the reader may ask. It's the American way, after all, but as I have learned, when the pursuit of success in this world overshadows or eliminates His role, it is not God's way. I thought I had attained so much, and I found I had actually attained very little on my own. My second lesson was in learning to recognize Who had given me the talents which led to my academic success and my success in the world of international business. I learned that the fruits of my success, the prestige, the promotions, and the material rewards, meant little in the eyes of God. Only He could transform my thinking and make me see the insignificance of material rewards; only he could make me see that when I stood before My Creator, all that really mattered was what I had given away.

I did not readily accept the idea that I had been given a second chance, a second "shot," at a spiritual life. I was too wrapped up in my own emotional pain to feel any great sense of joy, or offer any thanks for the fact that I was still among the living. It was much safer to dwell in denial, where I could pretend that all I experienced was a nightmare, where I could take comfort in rationalization, in the belief that soon I would wake up and return to the life I remembered. At the same time, my intellect forced me to come to terms with my reality, regardless of how horrible it seemed.

Intellect and acceptance prevailed eventually, but not before my hopelessness and helplessness were finally eroded by acceptance of God's great mercy. I overcame denial gradually, but my healing began with my acceptance. "This couldn't possibly be a dream," I argued, trying to maintain some semblance of sanity, on my better days. "The same people keep appearing in it, over and over again." These were people I wanted to cling to, such as my family, and people I wanted nothing to do with: the doctors, the nurses, and the therapists. "Who invited all these people into my life, anyway?" I raged inwardly and outwardly. "I want them out, and, fast!" Somehow, my ability to give orders never left me, but no one seemed to listen. Between my rage and my tears, I came to terms with the facts; although my legal blindness resulted directly from a hit-and-run accident, my spiritual blindness had occurred many years before. I learned that God moves a person's heart to seek change in accordance with His Will, and that one can not fight God; one cannot expect to change His Will. I learned to let Him lead.

My journey was a long one, but time has little meaning to God. I had to become a child again, so God could reach out and teach me His ways, remold me, rebuild me into what He desired. I was stripped of everything, so that He might fill me with everything He wanted to give me, molding me into the instrument He wanted me to be. I had to learn to deny myself, pick up my Cross, and follow Him, as Christ taught. I had rejected Him for some time, professing to know what was best for Joan. Slowly He filled me with a desire to rise above my pain and draw closer to Him. I am continually amazed at His patience in teaching me trust and obedience. With each fall I took, each borne of my pride and anger, He would pick me up, patiently pointing me in the right direction once again. I learned slowly to put my trust in a God who does not fail, for there was no other way for me to learn, except by taking the time to accept all the gifts God wanted to give me. I was stripped of everything I had been because God, in

His infinite wisdom, knew what was necessary for Him to reach this particular daughter.

"When God wishes to teach divine lessons to a soul, and speak to her heart, He leads her into the desert" (Hosea, 2:16.). In the many agonizing months of my rehabilitation, when I struggled to learn the simplest tasks over again, He showered me with His mercy, instilling in me a strength and obedience. I learned painfully and slowly. Through my trials and suffering, He taught me of His endless mercy, and He taught me the trust with which I needed to serve Him. Through my trials, through my suffering, God meant to purify and refine, as gold is refined in fire, until I was ready to be an instrument for the Hands of My Creator, to be used as He desired.

The inspiration to actually sit down, pick up a pen, and begin writing, came about slowly, in direct proportion to my own spiritual growth and awareness. This writing was not borne of myself; I was simply the instrument used to put the words down on paper. I can give no more concrete explanation; my purpose is not to explain, only to share.

This urge to share these events is not based on any personal intent to persuade the reader to my beliefs. I hold no false illusions that my words can convince anyone of the faith and beliefs to which I ascribe wholeheartedly. It is only God who convinces, and thus readers must draw their own conclusions regarding the content of this writing.

My work on this book has been complemented by invitations to speak, at churches (non-Catholic as well as Catholic), schools and universities, about my experiences since the accident. How did this happen? None of these activities was ever planned and yet they happen. This is how God works, never ceasing to confound man. We are all nothing more than instruments in God's Hands through which His Spirit flows, through which His Will is achieved.

I have no memory of the accident, and only vague recollections of the weeks and months that followed it. My doctors have said that I will never remember it, nor those initial weeks and months. God is kind that way, blocking the physical pain and much of the immediate trauma from my mind.

For details on the time immediately following the accident and for many months thereafter, I have relied upon my family, friends, medical and police reports. All have presented me with a gruesome picture. While I cringe at some of the more elaborate details, and imagine how awful it must have been, for my loved ones as well as for me, I take comfort in the recovery I have made to date, which the doctors had thought impossible, given the extent and uniqueness of my injury.

My recovery was a long and slow process, especially for someone who was so very much on the go, someone who tended to be a perfectionist. I always found it easier to accept others' limitations, than my own. I was continuously striving to be the best I could possibly be, in academics or in my career goals. It is ironic that I never applied that same attitude to the pursuit of spiritual goals. Now I realize how little Joan Ulicny did and achieved. All achievements, all true successes stem from God, for nothing succeeds like God, or without God. We are all but mere instruments through which His will is accomplished. I learned this at the height of my despair, I think, because God knew that was the only way I would come to reach out to Him.

In my need to achieve, I had forgotten that my accomplishments were not solely the result of my own talents and efforts. On the contrary, my most cherished achievements, whether at school or at work, resulted from the privilege of associating with, and learning from, remarkable and generous people — some of whom are mentioned in this writing. I vowed years ago, after finishing college and graduate school, to always remain a "student" during whatever course I might follow in life. Never did I hesitate to acknowledge those who played such vital roles in my life, teaching me and encouraging me in all my endeavors. Rather, my weakness, my downfall, was my failure to acknowledge the gifts and ever-ready assistance of Someone who loved me more than any other in existence, my Creator. Now I recognize Him as the Source of all my gifts, all my talents, and as the One Who has, and will, continue urging me to perfect them.

I am aware that these words will come as a surprise to those who knew me only as a woman who lived very much in the "real world," and seldom in the spiritual; I offer no explanations — except my surprise that these two worlds are so intricately connected, a fact I haven't always had the grace to see.

I am far from being a student of theology; I thrived on being a student of this world, and I always strove to better my position in it. It was unnecessary to dwell on the spiritual world, I thought. Today, after confronting all that has transpired in my life, particularly in these most recent years following the accident, I consider myself nothing more than an ordinary person, who, for reasons unknown to her, was blessed with some extraordinary experiences. My awareness slowly became acceptance, as I continued to struggle with my fears and anger, which were present even as I wrote these words; but my fear is not as great, and my anger no longer overwhelming. I understand now Who leads me, and I trust that He will continue to do so.

Mine is not a story of triumph over tragedy, but a story of reawakened faith. I pray that my story will give other women and men the courage to approach God.

PART ONE

"When God wishes to teach divine lessons to a soul, and speak to her heart, He leads her into the desert."

— Hosea 2:16

CHAPTER ONE

THE TIME BEFORE

I WAS BORN IN PITTSBURGH, PENNSYLVANIA, in February, 1957, on the 25th of the month. I am the eldest daughter of Rita and Joseph Ulicny, and I have one sister, Jean, four years younger than me. We grew up in a small neighborhood in Crafton Heights, about twenty minutes from Downtown Pittsburgh, and we both attended St. Philip's grade school and Canevin High School. I was an above-average student who wanted very much to further her formal education, and I never doubted that I would attend college. I entered Penn State University in 1975 and graduated in 1979 with a B.A. in Political Science. Not satisfied with ending my formal education at that time, I went on to earn a Master's degree in International Affairs, with a concentration in international business, from American University in Washington, D.C.

During my last year of graduate school, I successfully competed for a position as a co-op student at the Export Regulation Office of the IBM World Trade Corporation in Washington. The position lasted almost a year, and it allowed me to earn credit towards my Master's degree while gaining practical work experience in the business world. I was surprised at how much I enjoyed my position with IBM. Until that experience, I wanted to make my career with the U.S. State Department as a foreign service officer; I had already considered taking the Foreign Service Exam. A position as a foreign service officer would have allowed me to travel to foreign countries, a love I discovered during that final year of graduate school.

In 1980, I traveled to Europe to study the European Community with a group of students from American University. We traveled to Belgium, Luxembourg, Holland and France as the course of our studies took us to the headquarters of the European Community, the European Parliament, and to NATO headquarters. When our tour was completed, I stayed on in Europe to visit Switzerland and Italy. I traveled alone, staying at youth hostels, and was totally mesmerized by my solo adventure. I had an overwhelming desire to expand my overseas travel, and intended to make travel a part of my career.

After my experience with IBM, I knew that this was a company that encouraged its employees and worked to develop their talents. I wanted to be a permanent employee at IBM, but this goal wasn't easily or immediately accomplished. Although my manager was impressed with my skills and abilities, he informed me that there were no openings for permanent jobs in that particular IBM location. I then embarked on what seemed, at that time, to be the most difficult trial period of my life: my search for a career position that would provide me with a forum for developing and demonstrating my talents.

I was disappointed with the lack of opportunities available at IBM when I completed graduate school, and was eager to begin my career, but first I decided to fulfill a heart-felt desire that had been with me since my first trip to Europe: to travel to the Greek islands and see the ancient ruins. I had saved enough money from my co-op position with IBM and from a part-time waitressing job at a small Greek restaurant in D.C. to make the trip, and somehow I knew that this interlude between graduation and entrance into the responsibilities of the "real" world, the career-world, was the perfect opportunity to make this trip. So I journeyed to the Greek islands, travelling solo again. This was my adventure: I traveled to Athens, and then on to the islands of Naxos, Santorini, and Crete. I traveled alone, but felt no fear; I was fulfilling a dream.

Just before leaving the States, I learned that it was only an hour's flight from Athens to Tel Aviv, Israel. Immediately I thought, "What a wonderful opportunity to visit the Holy Land." I knew if I revealed this desire to my parents, their fears would ground me from ever leaving the States at all; they were anxious enough over my intention to travel alone in Greece. I decided they had enough to worry about, and I remained silent about my full plans. I did, however, discuss them with my friend and neighbor, Tommy, who had friends, Frank and Faye, living in Jerusalem at the time. He wrote and asked them to meet with me when I arrived there. Knowing my independent nature, he noted that I planned to stay in youth hostels and to visit certain places within the Holy Land. Frank and Faye wrote back, insisting that I stay with them, and I did, eventually; I spent my first two nights in a youth hostel which operated out of a convent, then I moved to the apartment they shared. Forewarned by Tommy on how I meant to use my time, they were gracious hosts, allowing me to stay in their apartment and use my days in Jerusalem to explore the Holy City. I rose early each day and signed up for trips to Bethlehem, Calvary, and the Dead Sea, all offered by local tour agencies. I often walked along The Via Dolorosa, the "Way of the Cross," and bought fruit at the local markets for my lunch, before continuing on with the Stations of the Cross. I bought a rosary, small pearls on a silver chain, with a silver crucifix, although I very rarely prayed with one. I explored, too, the holy shrines of other religions found in Jerusalem; I removed my shoes to enter the Holy Dome of the Rock, a place of devout worship for Muslims, and I stood next to Jews praying fervently at the Wailing Wall, watching silently as they placed written petitions in its cracks.

As a Catholic, I knew little of the Muslim and Jewish religions, but I had been raised to have a respect for all faiths. As I learned in the years ahead, it was, after all, not God who separated people; instead people separated themselves. As I think back to how I witnessed Arabs, Jews and Christians living and working together in Jerusalem, with each religion maintaining its own rites of worship, it is painful and difficult to acknowledge the violence and terrorism that rocks the Holy Land to this day.

As the days passed, I was full of excitement, anticipation, and awe because I walked the land where Christ lived and died. Still, in the back of my mind, I knew I needed to contact my parents and let them know my whereabouts. For all they knew, I was still in Greece. I had spoken to them last from Athens, giving no hint of my plans to visit Jerusalem. I finally phoned, collect, and I will never forget my father's voice. The operator said she had a collect phone call for Mr. or Mrs. Joseph Ulicny from their daughter Joan in Jerusalem. "Where?!" I heard my father say incredulously. Then he quickly added, "Yes, yes, I'll accept the charges." I don't remember the exact conversation, but I remember that his voice descended a few octaves when I told him that I was staying with friends of Tommy's in Jerusalem, and that I planned to return to the States within a week, flying directly to Pittsburgh. I tried to describe my need to travel to the Holy Land, but I'm not sure I succeeded — perhaps because I didn't fully understand it myself. I didn't go into details about my solo journeys to Bethlehem and through the streets of Jerusalem. After that call home, the last few days flew by, and soon I was back in the States.

I flew to Pittsburgh from Baltimore-Washington International airport, on the day Anwar Sadat was assassinated. I was anxious to see my parents, and conscious that they were anxious to see their vagabond daughter. My father hugged me and said, "I don't know whether I should hug you, or beat you." He settled for the hug and many, many kisses. My mother just kept kissing me and saying, "I should have never allowed you to venture beyond Barr Avenue," (the street where I grew up as a child). I chalked it up to another "Rita statement," the kind only she could deliver so well.   I stayed in Pittsburgh for over a week, visiting relatives and recounting my adventures in Greece and the Holy Land. I brought back vials of holy water and holy oil from Bethlehem, Christ's Tomb, Calvary, and the Garden of Gethsemane for my mother and grandmother. Little did I know then how treasured these vials of blessed oil and water would prove to us in the years to come. At that time, my trip made little impact on my life other than reaffirming my love of travel. I treasured my memories of the things I'd seen and experienced in the Holy Land, but spiritually I did very little with them.

I returned to Washington, D.C., in late October of 1981, exhilarated by my travel experiences, and anxious to pursue the job hunting I knew would lead me to that exciting career I had worked so hard for. While in Jerusalem, I prayed unceasingly for guidance; I prayed that I might be led to a career which would fully challenge and improve my talents. In Washington I turned all my energies to accomplishing that goal.

Regardless of what the Washington office had told me, I had submitted my resume and job application to various IBM employment offices before leaving for Greece and Israel. I received a letter from the Central Employment Office in D.C. which thanked me for my interest but said again that there were no openings for permanent positions requiring my skills at that time. My application would, however, stay on file for six months. Undaunted, I pressed on with my job search. I refused to be defeated by a few letters from IBM and other companies who were not hungry for my talents.

I returned to the waitressing job at the Greek restaurant. I worked nights to pay my rent and living expenses and kept my days free for job-hunting. I spent over two weeks on Capitol Hill alone, dropping off resumes at various Congressmen's and Senators' offices. I received no interviews or job offers. The hunting didn't get easier, and I was confronted daily by customers at the restaurant who would ask me, "Joanie, what are you still doing here?" "If only I knew," I thought. My confidence and determination were beginning to give way to despondency and weariness. I dreaded my weekly phone calls home, because I had nothing promising to tell my parents, and no solid job leads. My parents were always supportive, but I knew they were concerned about my despondency. Once I cried angrily into the phone, "Well, I guess it's just meant for me to be a waitress all my life!" At those times, I reflected on my time in Jerusalem. I had prayed so fervently for an answer to my career-search dilemma. But no answers appeared.

Then one day, in the summer of 1982, I received a phone call from Bill Kushner, my manager at IBM during my co-op position there. He told me of an opening for someone with U.S. Export Licensing experience at the IBM International Purchasing Office and Distribution Center in Poughkeepsie, New York, and he advised me to send a resume to Joe McGowan, Manager of the International Trade Programs department. I immediately sent the material to McGowan along with a cover letter. Within two weeks, I had a phone call from him, inviting me to New York for an interview. I spent a few hours with Joe, and I also met with his manager, Peter Idema, over lunch. I felt comfortable with these men, but I was constantly aware of this voice inside me screaming, "Did I get the job? Did I get the job?" After lunch, Joe and I went back to his office. He excused himself for a moment, which gave me more time to critique my interview with him. Had I appeared too anxious? Joe knew I was anxious for this job. It was difficult not to be; almost a year had passed since I had finished graduate school.

Joe returned to his office, closed the door, and formally offered me a position within his department as Export Licensing Coordinator. I was ecstatic, thanking him over and over again, until it was embarrassing. Finally, Joe leaned across his desk handed me his phone, and said, "Why don't you call your parents?" I did so, immediately. He left the room, graciously giving me some privacy. The minute I heard my mother's voice, I started yelling "I got the job, I got the job!" I had finally landed the career position I had worked so hard to attain. I returned to Washington, collected my things, bought a car, hung up my waitress apron forever, and put on my business suit and heels.

Adjusting to life in the business world was not difficult for me; I was hungry for its challenges. I excelled at my job, gaining confidence daily and looking constantly for ways to improve my job performance to the overall benefit of the company. I was committed to the organization I worked for, but I was also very much aware that, as the new kid on the block, I had a lot to learn before I would be in a position to initiate ideas and plans that could make a difference. Eventually I did enter an area where I could initiate and implement changes as well as direct their route to fruition.

After only two years with IBM, I was promoted into management, which, as I was to learn, was quite an achievement for someone with so little time with the company. Despite some initial problems during my first year of management, I overcame misperceptions by becoming even more diligent in my efforts to move my entire department toward the recognition it sorely needed, both as a team and as individuals. Managers must develop their own particular styles of management; mine was based on commitment, and on the drive to confront problems and work to resolve them. Similarly, no one handed out style with the title of "manager"; instead one acquired it in the course of daily management decisions; I did a lot of learning in my first year of management.

Just as I'd hoped, my position indulged my love affair with foreign travel. As a World Trade Manager, I gave presentations at IBM locations in Argentina, Brazil, Canada, Mexico, Korea, and Japan. Only in my mid-twenties, this "kid" from Pittsburgh truly lived a dream — a dream that came to a shocking halt on December 2, 1986.

A GREATER VISION

CHAPTER TWO

THE ACCIDENT

The following narrative is based on the police accident report, on medical documentation, and, most importantly, on the recollections of my family and friends. I have no memory of the events surrounding my accident or the initial stages of my recovery. Much later, I asked the people who surrounded me with love and support during those first few months to write down their memories of the accident, and I've depended on their stories, as well as the ones my parents told me, to piece together what happened. My sister Jeanie, Michael Grasso — the very special man in my life at the time of the accident, who shared with me excerpts from the diary he kept in those initial days and weeks — and Sister Mary Agnes McCormick, O.L.C., provided me with a great deal of help. I am forever indebted to their generosity and love, which allowed them to submit their words and recollections describing this time of pain and anxiety that, perhaps, they preferred not to recall.

I LEFT MY PARENTS' HOME IN PITTSBURGH early that day, beginning the long drive back to the Hudson Valley in New York, where I lived, and where I worked for IBM. My dog, Peanut, was travelling with me, and he was the primary reason I chose to drive, rather than fly, home. I hated the thought of putting Peanut in an airline carrier, and preferred having him with me at all times. I usually stopped several times throughout the seven hour trip to relax and walk him. It was a long but leisurely drive and, for the most part, relaxing. I never imagined that this particular trip would be anything else. My accident occurred at approximately 9:30 that morning, when I collided with an 18-wheeler.

On December third, the day after the accident, my father received a phone call from the driver of the 18-wheeler which had hit me head-on; he was distraught as he told his version of the accident. The driver said that I attempted to pass a truck on I-80 and correctly signaled my intent to do so, but the driver of the truck I was passing suddenly pulled out without warning and bumped my car off the road. My car immediately went into a spin, and I lost control. The driver of the 18-wheeler began pumping his brakes, watching me spin ahead of him. He told my father that he was afraid of locking his brakes, jack-knifing his truck, and crushing me. I drove a white Honda Prelude, hardly a match for his truck. As fate would have it, when he finally locked his brakes, I spun out directly in front of him, and our two vehicles met head-on. The driver informed my father that he radioed ahead to the other truck driver, saying that he "had just knocked that white four-wheeler off the road." The driver reportedly responded, "What car, what car?" and he stated that there were "no marks on his vehicle." He then suggested that the driver of the 18-wheeler pull off at the next exit so they could "discuss it."

The driver could see me in the car, but he couldn't open the car to reach me. Even after help arrived, he said, "time seemed actually longer than it was because of the emotions and trauma and standing and watching [her] suffer." It took over an hour for an emergency crew to extract me from my car, and the driver estimated that the police arrived about twenty minutes after the emergency crew. I have no recollection of any part of this. The driver and other witnesses said that I was awake at the scene of the accident, but I lost consciousness somewhere after I was extracted from my car and before arriving at Clarion Hospital.

When they finally freed me from the wreck, I was rushed by ambulance to Clarion Hospital, where the emergency staff almost immediately decided that my injuries were too severe for their facilities. Already it was evident that my head injuries were extensive. Their records showed that I stopped breathing, one clear indication of brain injury. I was revived and taken by ambulance once again to Allegheny General Hospital in Pittsburgh, site of the nearest Hospital Trauma Unit. Clarion alerted the Allegheny Trauma team, and there I was met by Dr. Dan Diamond who headed the Trauma Unit.

Dr. Diamond:

Things began to happen before [Joan] arrived ... in her case, we were notified ahead of time ... our Life Dispatcher notifies a team of surgical personnel, which includes a surgeon, a senior resident, a junior resident, two interns, radiologist resident and staff person, anesthesiologist and resident, two nurse anesthetists, blood bank, operating room and several other entities within the hospital. The team [was] present in the receiving room ... available the minute [she] hit the door. The team examined [Joan] upon arrival. She was restrained on a back board, there was a decreased level of consciousness, which had been noted in the ambulance en route to the hospital.

Previously she had some trouble with breathing, but no problem with blood pressure ... At the time she arrived, she had a breathing tube in place because ... she had not been breathing just before she was presented to the other hospital. She had some bruises and her pupils were not equal, they reacted to light but they were somewhat sluggish in their reaction. The fact that they were unequal is suggestive that either the eye was injured or one side of the brain may have been injured ... She was — she responded only to pain ... That means that if you spoke to her or yelled at her or tried to ask her to do something for you like raise a finger, squeeze your hand, she would not respond to that. It ... goes along with having a severe head injury. She moved only when

> *you did something that caused pain, and then her*
> *body would respond almost without — in a sense*
> *without the upper brain functions. She underwent*
> *... a series of x-rays ... and a mini operation on the*
> *abdomen, which did not indicate any internal inju-*
> *ries. She had a head scan as well.*

Hours after the accident, around 3:30 in the afternoon, a social worker from Allegheny General Hospital in Pittsburgh contacted my parents at home. As my parents learned later, my employer knew of the accident almost immediately after it occurred, because I carried my IBM I.D. badge in my purse. I had no identification that indicated my family ties to Pittsburgh. Through IBM, the social worker obtained my parents' address and phone number. She told them only that I was in the trauma unit of Allegheny General Hospital in Pittsburgh, and that I had been in an auto accident.   After some initial confusion by the Admissions Staff at Allegheny — they were unsure whether or not I had been admitted as a patient — my parents met a Dr. Fitzpatrick who confirmed that I was there. He told them that my right leg was severely broken and that I was in a coma. Allegheny General medical reports indicated that I had a trauma scale of +8 and a coma scale of +10, significant information for those in charge of my medical care, but of little meaning or comfort to my parents.

Months later, Dr. Diamond explained that the coma scale was a way of grading head injuries; the best possible score was 15 and 3 was the worst. Almost all patients who are graded 3 die, and most with a 6 or below die. It is unusual for patients with scores in the lower half to survive or regain their normal life functions. I was borderline, and my condition was deteriorating.

My parents were told only that I had been involved in an auto-truck collision on Interstate 80, and was initially taken to Clarion Hospital, which was nearest the site of the accident. More details slowly trickled in over the next few days, but my family had little time and attention for collecting them at that time. The severity and extent of my injuries wasn't clear to them for several days.

Apparently Michael was notified soon after the wreck as well. My secretary at IBM, Diane Coghlan, contacted him. His account is based on his journal.

Michael:

I was in my office in New Jersey, and had called Poughkeepsie to review some future appointments with patients I had there. When I called Diane [your secretary], your manager, Chris, said, "I have some bad news — Joan was in an accident." From the sound of his voice, I knew that it was bad. He told me that you were in Pittsburgh. I got the number and immediately started calling. I was put in touch with the Trauma Center. You had not yet been admitted there, so they put me in touch with the emergency room. I got your nurse in the emergency room. She put the phone up to your ear, and I started screaming, "Joan! Joan!" I was frantic. I then managed to get your parents. They had just arrived, and I asked them what had happened. They were uncertain of the details.

Then I asked, "Where's Peanut?" They had forgotten about your dog, and I told them that I would find out. I started calling the State Trooper barracks up and down Route 80. I had a sketchy idea of what had happened. You had been taken, first, to Clarion Hospital. I managed to get the State Trooper barracks that had been summoned to the scene of your accident. I got the State Trooper — the one who had first got to you. His name was Wolinski. He told me about the accident — what apparently had happened. I asked him what you had said when he got to you, and he said that you kept saying, "Get me out of here!" Some time from the time they were extracting you from the car to the point of putting you in the ambulance, you went unconscious. And at Clarion Hospital you stopped breathing.

> *He told me that he had left Peanut with an in-*
> *tern at Clarion. He gave me her phone number, and*
> *I called her all night long. Finally, she got home and*
> *she confirmed that, yes, she did have Peanut. She*
> *gave me some more information about you, and she*
> *said that you weren't doing so well. She spoke about*
> *the pupils of your eyes, which were an indication of*
> *your brain damage.*

At the hospital, my parents saw me only a few minutes before I was taken into surgery to set my broken right
femur. They entered my room to find me attached to all
kinds of machinery: a heart monitor, a respirator/ventila-
tor, and life-support. I was also undergoing blood trans-
fusions; records show that I took a total of seven pints of
blood that day. The imprint of my shoulder strap was visible across my chest, indicating my body thrust against
the strap in the impact of the crash. According to my parents, the imprint remained for days.

I can only imagine their horror at the sight of their
daughter lying there so totally incapacitated. After that
shock, my parents met the doctor in a small room, where
they answered a number of questions about my personal
health. Because the pupils of my eyes were dilated, the
doctors needed to know if I was taking medication, using
other drugs, or if I was pregnant. My parents insisted that
the answer to all of these questions was negative.

My father contacted my eye doctor in New York, Dr.
Praeger, confirming that I no longer used an eye drop medication prescribed for me following eye surgery, performed
in 1986 for a detached retina, the result of an earlier accident. Dr. Praeger told my father that dilated pupils were an
indication of brain injury due to this latest accident.

The emotional battle my parents underwent at this
time is incomprehensible to me. They were told that surgery on my right leg must be done immediately to relieve
my traumatized brain from the excruciating pain of my
broken leg. So much was thrown at them so quickly; there
was no time for detailed discussion or explanation in the
trauma unit, where time is a critical factor in saving lives.

My leg was so badly broken, the surgeon commented to my parents that he was amazed the bone hadn't come through the flesh. I underwent three and a half hours of surgery on December second. A split pin, a stainless steel rod, was inserted into my right leg and attached to two screws which were mounted near my right hip, and another two which were mounted near my right knee. The surgery went well, according to the surgeon who met with my parents briefly afterward. He indicated, however, that given the severity of the break, I might require a cane when walking, and that I might walk with a limp.

Following the surgery on my leg, medical records indicate that I showed no signs of increasing responsiveness; in fact, I showed minimal response. Medical records state that I showed an increased temperature and a decreased mental status, responding only to pain. Another CAT scan revealed a fracture to my left maxillary sinus which resulted from the pressure of my eyeglasses against my cheekbone upon collision impact. This fracture was set without incident, and my fever subsided.

The initial CT scan taken on December second showed no evidence of intercranial bleeding, but it did show acute infarction to the right parietal/occipital area and the left occipital area of my brain. In these areas, brain tissue was dying or dead, due to a lack of blood and oxygen. This CT scan provided the initial indication of brain damage, but no one discussed specific brain damage, or its results, with my parents at that time.

Increasingly concerned about my decreased level of consciousness, the trauma team consulted among themselves, then told my parents they wanted to conduct an angiogram. The doctors suspected that there might be a problem with the arteries in my neck that carry blood and oxygen to the brain; damage to these arteries might explain my decreased consciousness and lack of response to anything but pain. The doctors also explained that such a procedure carried some risks. My brain had undergone such tremendous trauma from the accident that injecting any additional substance into my body could add increased pressure to the brain, and thus kill me. My father told me that he simply looked at the neurosurgeon and asked, "If she were your daughter, what would you do?" The neurosurgeon again made clear the dangers of an angiogram: It could leave me a vegetable or kill me. But the gravity of the situation was that I "was slipping away." I "was going to die, anyway," he told my father. My father consented to the angiogram, signed the release form, then went to the hospital chapel to pray with my mother. Sometime that night they called my sister, Jeanie.

Jeanie:

Dad called me late on December 2, 1986, to let me know about the accident and that you had a broken leg. I had an interview with Fidelity (Investments) two days later, so he didn't tell me the extent of your injuries. On Wednesday, December 3, 1986, you were scheduled for an angiogram, and I knew I had to come home. I canceled the interview and was home at eight. I met Dad and Michael at the airport and went to the intensive care unit at Allegheny General Hospital. Upon seeing you, the only thing I could liken it to was one of our older relatives who had died, and was laid out in one of those horrible funeral homes. I was afraid to touch you, afraid that you might be cold, just like the corpses of those old women relatives. Grandpap was there, crying; it was the first time I had ever seen him cry. Mom was in shock, racing around like she always does, in perpetual motion. Dad was shell-shocked, and going through the motions. I felt compelled to keep composure — they needed me to be strong, and so I was. You would sometimes move your feet, and we'd be so happy. Then you would retch with pain and cry. But that was better than seeing you cough and open your eyes, only for us to see those once full-of-life huge blues, dead and lacking of any promise. That is what hit me the most — the lack of life and energy for which we all depended on you. This was something completely out of our hands.

Michael:

Finally, your sister arrives [at the airport, where my father met him and Jeanie], and we go to the car. We get to the hospital, your father drops your sister and me off at the entrance. We are permitted to see you, even though it is after visiting hours. We walk into the room, and I start crying. Your sister walks over to the bed, and I leave to go into the bathroom, and cry. The nurse follows me in, and asks me if I am all right. I tell her that I am a dentist, and, look at me — at how I am reacting. I go back into the room, walk right over to the bed, and know exactly what I am going to say to you. You always told me that you wouldn't leave, one minute before your time. You said that was what Anwar Sadat always said to his wife. I go over to the bed, hold your hand, and say, "Joan, it's not time." You arch your back, and move around as if you wanted to get out of bed. Your father explains to me, later, that this was the most movement you had shown in 24 hours.

When I heard Michael's account of the accident, recognizing the words I so often said to him brought back some of the more intimate conversations we had shared. Michael and I were friends, and I think I shared with him more of my deeper thoughts than I had ever shared with anyone. I can remember, though somewhat vaguely, how much I admired Anwar Sadat before the accident, and that I once saw his widow, Jihan Sadat, interviewed by Barbara Walters on a television special. Ms. Walters asked her how she had been able to live her life in the face of the death threats that often came to her husband, particularly after he re-established relations with Israel despite the vocal opposition from other Arab states and within his own country.

I remember how calm and confident Mrs. Sadat was in giving her reply. She simply stated that her husband had said, "Jihan, don't you know that I will not go one moment before my time?" I found that comment so inspiring that I had adopted it into my own life. I began to believe, strongly, that God knew from the moment a person was born just how much time that person was allotted in this life, and that there was nothing an individual could do to change that predetermined destiny. With this realization came a feeling of peace about death, not fear. Michael remembered my words to him, taken from Sadat, and, I think now, that even while lying in that hospital bed, comatose, I must have heard him and responded.

The wait for the results of the angiogram seemed endless, according to my parents; They were anxious for the results, but they feared the outcome. They sat second-guessing their decision, afraid it was the wrong one. It was, as my father explained many months later, the most difficult decision he or my mother ever had to make, one that would affect every member of our family for the rest of their lives. Whatever the outcome, we'd all have to live with it — in my case, perhaps not live at all. The outcome "was not in our hands," my father said. The angiogram was conducted on December third, 1986, and the results startled and confounded the trauma team.

That evening my mother, accompanied by Jeanie, met with Dr. Diamond, the head of the Allegheny General Trauma Unit, to discuss the results. My father went to the airport to meet a friend who had flown in to see me. What the angiogram showed astonished the doctors of the trauma team, for it revealed that all four of the arteries in my neck, those that carry blood and oxygen to the brain, were clotted. One was completely occluded. Dr. Diamond drew a sketch of the neck arteries to help explain the problem to my sister and mother.

Dr. Diamond:

> *It is unusual to have damaged arteries in the neck without having a broken jaw or a broken neck, but in her case, we were shocked and horrified to see that all four of the neck vessels that supply the brain*

were actually injured. One of them was occluded, that is, it was shut off, it had clotted off, the other three all had injuries within the wall, which had resulted in narrowing and presumably the stroke or the dead area of brain had occurred because blood clots on the very injured surface of the artery developed and then flipped off and went up into the brain and lodged, blocking a small artery that supplied a piece of the brain ... These are extremely rare cases, in fact, I know of no case like this one that has ever been written about anywhere ... We then had two choices: One was to try and operate upon those vessels, which would not recover the brain function and might well [be] fatal [because] it might extend the problem in the brain. One of the vessels could not have been operated on in any extent — two ... of the four actually. The other two would have been very dangerous and difficult operations, even had she not had a stroke already. The other alternative to an operation was to thin her blood, which we were concerned about doing because of her recent broken bones, the possibility of other injuries, and the fact that she might bleed into the dead area of the brain.

We took the alternative that seemed the least risky for her ... to try to thin her blood, to try to prevent any further clots from traveling to the brain ...

One clot had already gone to my brain, where it had apparently caused a stroke. My entire left side was paralyzed. My injury was the first of its kind, and my family was told that it was the doctors' experience that a person with two clotted neck arteries did not survive; yet I lay in coma, still alive, with clots in all four arteries (one of my doctors later wrote a medical paper which underlined the severity and uniqueness of my injury). The doctors could rely on no documented, prescribed course of treatment to increase my chances for survival. Dr. Diamond explained to my mother and sister that there was no way to prevent another clot from causing further damage, or death. I was placed on heparin, a blood thinning medication, via a blood thinning machine, but no treatment could guarantee protection from another stroke. My sister told me that Dr. Diamond then looked at her and my mother, and he said if there were any place he could send me, anywhere in the world I might get the help I needed to increase my chances of survival, he would tell them immediately. But at the moment all they could do was pray — that was the only hope he offered my family. My mother said they just sat there in shock. What did he mean that there was no documented course of treatment to follow that would guarantee her daughter's life? Allegheny General was one of the finest trauma centers in the country — they had to know how to help, how to ensure my survival. These thoughts raced through my mother's mind: I had already survived so much against the odds — the impact of the crash itself, the hours it took to extract me from the car, the ambulance ride from Clarion to Allegheny General, the comatose days, and the angiogram itself. My mother told me she prayed: "Surely, You're not going to take her from me now, are You?" I had survived trauma after trauma, only to reach a point where my family heard that prayer was their only hope.

How hopeless these words must have sounded at that time; how hollow and devoid of hope they sounded as I wrote them. But little could any of us have known then, the extent of hope that those words offered. Prayer was all that was left, but prayer would prove enough. My family prayed, placing their trust in God, knowing that a call might come at any time, notifying them of my death.

Immediately following their conversation with Dr. Diamond, Jeanie contacted a friend of hers who was far more experienced in the medical field than anyone in our family. Michael Copley had been involved in a serious accident, years earlier, and he too was not expected to live. Michael contacted another friend, a doctor in California who, in turn, called Dr. McGovern, Director of Allegheny General Hospital. Dr. McGovern made a personal visit to my room in the trauma unit the following day. My parents said that his visit caused a flurry of activity among both doctors and nurses, one of whom was heard to exclaim, "Oh my, Dr. McGovern. He never comes down here." Before he left the floor, he told the nurses he wanted to see all my films and records on his desk immediately, and he wanted to see Dr. Diamond as soon as he got in to the hospital.

Jeanie:

I called Michael Copley that day [December third]; he called Jim Maloney, the head surgeon at UCLA, a friend of ours. Michael Copley discussed you with Jim and then called me back to tell me that there was little hope.

An injury such as yours was never registered. The four clotted arteries were the big issue. You could go at any time, and so we waited. I couldn't tell Mom; I told Dad, so he could prepare her for the worst. We were so concerned about her; her worst nightmare, that one of her "beautiful and perfect" babies was harmed, was now a horrible and devastating reality. How would she deal with it? Jim Maloney said you were in the best trauma unit in the country. You began to stabilize over the next few days, and I could tell that you were still in the game. You were fighting, but you were scared and wanted Mom. Although in a coma, I think you must have known that we were all there — you just couldn't talk. You were still connected to life support systems and were being fed through an N.G. [a nasal-gastronomical tube]. During that first week, the doctors talked about comas, brain injuries, and the next steps. But before I forget, I want to describe the waiting room to you. It was morbid. There was an awful room off of the waiting room where they took the families of the patients who were just about to die. We saw several go in and out. How Mom blocked that out, I'll never know. It's amazing — you can fear something to the point where you are convinced that you could never handle it and then the human spirit prevails, and you get through it. Mom, especially, is proof of that.

About this time, Dad and Michael Grasso went to get your personal belongings from your car. It had been towed from the site of the accident, and had been impounded by the State Police. Michael said that Dad had finally broken down; I think the injustice of it all had finally got to him. He is such a straight-shooter. He just couldn't comprehend something like this happening to his family.

Michael:

After lunch your father and I set out to get Peanut, out near Clarion Hospital, and to see your car. When we get to the place where your car had been towed, I ask your father if he wants me to go ahead, first. He insists upon going with me. I'm afraid that he might have a nervous breakdown. I'm afraid to let him see the car. He insists on going. We go to the car, and I run up to see how badly damaged it is. I get right in the car, and start pulling things out of it. I jump in the driver's seat, just to see how much room you had. It appeared that you had some room. You have such long legs. I think you drive with your knees bent. When the truck hit you, the console was pushed in on you, and that was how your leg was broken. Fortunately, you did not have a passenger. If you had, the passenger would definitely have been killed. The passenger seat was totally crushed. We left to go and get Peanut. The internist finally gets off of her shift. Your father goes into the men's room and finally breaks down. I don't know what to do.

I go into the lobby, and start reading the Bible. We leave to pick up Peanut. We get to Clarion Hospital, and I call Allegheny General to see how you are doing. No change. We get Peanut, and he is elated. Your father gets a kiss from Peanut, and the internist starts to cry.

I drive home. Your father sits in the back seat with Peanut. Peanut cries all the way home. Your father starts telling me what a wonderful daughter you are, and what a wonderful child you were. I tell him how much I love you. We go back to Allegheny General Hospital. You are pretty active. At times, you had been so still. My uncle (also a doctor) said that you were probably very heavily sedated.

Sister Mary Agnes, who serves at Holy Trinity Catholic Church in Robinson Township, the parish to which my parents belong, learned of my accident and came to the hospital. She was a God-send to my family in those early months.

Sister Agnes:

My first recollection of Joan Ulicny began with a phone call to me from a neighbor of Mr. and Mrs. Ulicny, Mrs. Erin Zeh. She began by telling me of Joan's accident, and that Joan was in a coma at Allegheny General Hospital in Pittsburgh. My initial reaction was one of horror and I thought, "Is she going to live long enough for the priests and me to come and see her?" I then called the trauma ICU of Allegheny General and asked to speak to any family member available. It so happened, that Joan's sister, Jeanie, answered the phone. I told her who I was, and asked her how Joan was doing. She amazed me with her concise summary of the accident, how Joan even survived, how her parents were, and the exact time of visiting hours. She also related how long Joan had been there, and how the parents were waiting for the latest reports from the doctors. I assured her of our prayers, and told her that the priests would be coming in soon. She seemed most grateful for the phone call and told me that she would convey our concern to her parents.

The next day, Fathers Bob, Andy and I went to visit Joan. We went into the ICU somewhat appre-

hensively, as we did not know what to expect. There lay Joan, unconscious, with tubes north, east, south and west, in a somewhat upright position, 'sitting' almost in a wheelchair. As we moved closer, we noticed that she was strapped into the chair. She was the only one in the room, and there was soft music playing in the background. We looked at her for a long while, and none of us said a word. It was almost as if our speech would disturb her.

Then Fathers Bob and Andy began to pray over her, and give her their blessings. It was quite a beautiful, uplifting sight to see these two priests lift their hands over Joan's head and ask God to bestow His special blessing upon her. When they finished, I bent down over her and cupped her face in my hands, and asked the Blessed Mother to help her. At that moment, Joan's eyes fluttered! I brought this to the attention of both priests. I attribute this sign to their priestly blessing. When we got home, I called Mr. Ulicny to let him know that we had been to see Joan, and told him what had happened. The next day when Mr. and Mrs. Ulicny went to see Joan, the nurse informed them that Joan was showing signs of awakening from the coma. We still marvel to this day, at this miraculous occurrence.

I did not fully awake from the coma for 18 days. This time was emotionally draining for my family as they hurried out to the trauma unit to hold my hand and talk with me, although I was not responsive. To them, it seemed physically and emotionally impossible to take the logical and necessary steps to begin the investigation into the events that brought me to the point of near-death. Slowly, however, the pieces and the players were collected for my family, forming another horrible and illogical cross to bear in this unfolding nightmare.

The police report filed states that the driver of the truck that initially bumped me off the road was "not at the scene of the accident." I was apparently the victim of a hit-and-run accident. The police report, dated 12-2-86, states the following:

> *As Unit One was travelling on the right lane of I-80 East, Unit Two [my car] approached from behind in the left lane. As Unit Two was alongside the rear of the trailer of Unit One, Operator One began changing lanes, moving into the left lane. The left rear of the trailer made contact with the right side of Unit Two. Operator Two was forced off the roadway onto the northern berm. At this time, Operator Two applied the brakes and lost control of Unit Two. Unit Two spun out across the roadway. As Unit Three approached the scene, Unit Two was out of control, facing the flow of traffic. Operator Three was unable to avoid a collision with Unit Two. Unit Three struck the right front of Unit Two head-on. Upon this operator's arrival at the scene, Unit Two was at its final resting position in the left lane facing northwest, three feet onto the northern berm. Unit Three was moved prior to arrival onto the southern berm. Unit One was not at the scene. Debris from the impact of Units Two and Three was scattered along the right lane and southern berm. A black strip of side molding from the right side of Unit Two was located on the northern berm, approximately 315 feet from the final resting position of Unit Two. Tire impressions were observed in the snow along the northern berm approximately 300 feet from the final resting position of Unit Two. The impressions were approximately one foot off the road — way onto the north berm and extended for 15 feet. A black streak mark was observed on the right side door of Unit Two. Black tire rubbing marks were observed over the right front hubcap of Unit Two. Traces of white paint were imbedded into the black strip of side molding. Green, blue, yellow paint chips were observed on the right front fender of Unit Two. Damage to Unit Two was severe with major impact occurring on the right front*

*side. Damage to Unit Three was light. Front bumper
was dented. Operator One was not at the scene.*

*Operator Three was interviewed at the scene of
the accident and stated the following: that he was
proceeding east on I-80. He observed a white four-
wheeler (Unit Two) in the left lane jam on the brakes.
It appeared that the tractor trailer, (Unit One) travelling in the right lane, pulled out into the left lane
from the right lane. The four-wheeler lost control of
the car, went towards the median, across roadway
to the right lane spinning around. "I applied my
brakes, nowhere to go. I hit the four wheeler (Unit
Two) in the right lane. Prior to the accident, Unit
One passed my vehicle. I observed that he did not
have his headlights on ... I contacted Operator One
on the CB radio to inform him about his headlights.
The operator responded 'Thank-you.' After the accident occurred, I got on the CB radio and stated to
Operator One that 'you just hit the four-wheeler.' He
responded saying, 'What four-wheeler?' I stated, 'The
one trying to pass you.' He responded saying, 'I didn't
see any car and don't have any marks on my unit.
Switch over to channel 15 so we can talk.' At this
time, I got out of my vehicle to assist Operator Two."*

The police report confirmed the story the driver originally told my father. Our lives had been irrevocably
changed by a hit-and-run auto/truck accident. Now it was
up to my family and me to put the pieces of our lives back
together again, none of us knowing what the future might
hold, none of us sure I would even be a part of that future.

Although I was still in the last stages of coma, Dr. Diamond tried to examine and measure my eyesight. The results of the CAT scan, which suggested damage in the occipital area of my brain, and my behavior, implied that
my vision had been affected. On December 16, he consulted with a neuro-ophthalmologist, Dr. Kennerdell, who
examined me and confirmed that I "appeared to have a
severe visual loss."

As I slowly emerged from the coma, it was clear to everyone around me that I'd lost a lot — for how long, my family weren't sure. According to my parents, I could recognize and respond to my family, but I couldn't speak clearly, and my short term memory was damaged. I had some movement on the right side of my body, and less on the left side, which had been damaged by the stroke.

Michael returned home on December the fifth, four days after the accident. He recorded on a cassette tape the experiences he had written down during those initial days. I imagine that he must have wondered whether I would ever get to hear it. As of February 5th, 1989, I was still unable to read his log independently.

He visited me once or twice in the months after the accident, and at the end of the tape he also described a few "highlights" — things that made me laugh, things that only Michael could get away with telling me — from those times. That part of our relationship had not changed. I think we often competed to try and get the last word in; this time I prevailed.

He described talking to me in the early days after I awoke from the coma: One day he sat beside me and told me that I was "an intelligent lady," and I replied without hesitation, "Yes, I am." Perhaps that response, more than anything, was a sign of my increased awareness and consciousness. I don't remember these visits. Commenting on my sister, I said that Jeanie "gave me a headache," hardly an unlikely comment from me. Michael recalled that he asked me where I lived, and I replied, "Alabama." Why? I have no idea. I've never even been to Alabama.

But this tape essentially ends what Michael shared with me. It still hurt, two years later, to hear his voice. I still miss him very much, and I miss how we were together. But that time seems long ago, and so much has changed for both of us. Our relationship simply wasn't strong enough to bear the violent change the accident initiated in my life. I couldn't say to him, "Don't worry. I'm still the same person," because I knew I was not; it was not the handicaps that mattered, but a deeper, internal difference that evolved slowly, that had everything to do with spiritual change, something I did not think possible for me. As I began a program of physical and cognitive rehabilitation, spiritual rehabilitation was the furthest thing from my mind. God, however, knew what I needed the most.

Jeanie:

Gloria Williams came to visit after Michael Grasso returned to his parents' home in New Jersey. She was great! We bought you a tape deck, and started playing it for you. We played the "Big Chill" tape, and started dancing with you. It was comical relief. The only problem was that you kept trying to lead from your bed.

Then the doctors began talking about how this was going to be a very long process, referring to recovery, and how you were going to need us more in six months than now, so we had all better start taking care of ourselves. I had to return to Boston to interview again with Fidelity Investments. I remember that Mom, Dad and I went to Eat 'n Park, and I suggested that they should have other people to talk to. But they disagreed. They are such private people, and they said that they could handle it themselves. Around the 23rd of December, you began coming out of coma — just in time for Christmas. We missed you so much on Christmas Eve. I started crying, then Dad did, but Mom kept strong. I guess we all wanted to pretend that it was all a bad dream. I didn't have the job at Fidelity, yet. It was a bad holiday. Now they were talking about recovery and brain damage. You were transferred to Harmarville Rehabilitation Center — a horrible place. Seeing you this time was many times worse than seeing you on December third. You looked like Joan, but the area in your neck where the trache tube had been made noise when you tried to talk, and your voice sounded like a chipmunk's. It was then, that I was able to see what the accident had done to you. You were not my "big sister," only a skeleton of what she once was. I was very frightened by this, and I honestly did not know if I could handle it. I kept saying, "Thank God she is alive, but what a road ahead of her. Could she do it? Would you ever accept yourself as less than you had been?" But, of course, I fell in love with you all over again. It was a different role for me. Mom, again, so strong.

Christmas, 1986. Michael Copley came to visit. He came and went. He sent 29 poinsettia plants. We all gave you gifts, but you couldn't remember. It was funny. Again, it was comic relief. We were all on autopilot. You showed some of your old self towards the end of January, 1987 — p.o.'d at being dependent. It was reassuring to see that.

Michael Copley had talked to Frank Clark, his father-figure, in Los Angeles. Frank is a very successful lawyer in L. A., and head of the Board of Regents. Through Frank Clark, the name of attorney Paul Moses, in Pittsburgh, was obtained. Mom and Dad met with Mr. Moses, and he agreed to take your case.

My parents, primarily at the urging of my sister and Michael Copley, decided to file a lawsuit against the driver of the truck that originally ran me off the road, initiating my accident. Eventually, the case was settled, but it was some time — years — before I was able to resolve my own rage, my own resentment against this injustice, and continue on the journey God had set for me.

Sister Agnes:

I kept in contact with Joan's family, and learned that she was transferred to Harmarville Rehabilitation Center. Father Andy and I went to visit her there. It is quite a large place, and we had to walk "cross country" to finally locate her room. I remember that when I first walked into Joan's room, I was surprised to find that she was not there. We learned from a nurse that she was in therapy, and so we waited in her room. As we were sitting there, my eyes scanned the room, and I was so very impressed by all the cards, flowers, gifts and stuffed animals gracing the room. It made me think of a person who was well loved by her fellow workers, friends and family. This would be the first time I'd be seeing Joan since she had awakened from her coma, and I was anxious to see what her personality was like. Joan's mother then came in; it was also the first time I would meet her. Joan finally returned from therapy, and her mother wheeled her into the room. Father Andy and I both stood up, and her mother introduced Joan to us. We both kissed her and embraced her. Her first words were, "Oh, how do you do? I'm so happy you came to visit me."

I looked down to see a most beautiful-looking girl, who had the charm and social graces of one who had been well-trained both at school and in her job. Her mother went on to explain to her how we had been to see her at Allegheny General, and that we had prayed over her there. Her mother also explained what had happened while we had prayed. Joan then said, "Oh, thank you both so very much for that. I'm sure that is what pulled me through."

We did not talk about the accident, but rather centered on her physical therapy at Harmarville. I was quite impressed with Joan's strong will to overcome her injuries. It was so wonderful to see someone who really was a "miracle to be alive," and one who was a true answer to so many prayers.

CHAPTER THREE

REALITY SETS IN

I WAS TRANSFERRED to the Harmarville Rehabilitation Center on December 20, 1986 as an in-patient. My family was adamant about moving me before the Christmas holiday. They were increasingly distraught over the condition they often found me in during the designated visiting hours in Allegheny General's ICU. Often they found me sitting alone in my wheelchair, strapped in so I couldn't slide out. Sometimes they found me lying in the "mat room," left there so I could roll around and experience some type of physical movement. This provided me with some exercise without allowing me to harm myself. I don't remember the mat room, and I'm grateful for that.

Preserving my dignity didn't concern those who watched and aided my battle for life and awareness in those initial weeks. Still, hearing stories of the mat room, or hearing that my right hand was tied to the bed to prevent me from pulling out my trache tube, caused me to cringe. Human pride can be a strong motivator in overcoming physical obstacles, just as it can be a great deterrent in overcoming spiritual handicaps.

At that point in my recovery, I was conscious and aware of my surroundings, but my memory was extensively damaged. I recognized my old friends and my family, and I could respond to people and carry on a conversation, but I quickly forgot what we said and did. For instance, I don't remember my first meeting with Sister Agnes; our friendship didn't really begin to grow until many months later. Like dreams, my memories of that time are vague and fragmented, although some are more vivid than others.

For a long time, my family seemed to appear and disappear. I have one clear memory of that Christmas holiday in 1986: One of the activities planned for patients and their families at Harmarville during the holidays was bingo, which was held in the cafeteria. I can vaguely remember sitting in my wheelchair with a bingo card in front of me and hearing a man's voice call out various numbers: B-15, N-64. I distinctly remember my sister looking up from her bingo card at me and saying in a voice laced with sarcasm — but with some seriousness as well — "I'll never forgive you for this, Joan." I don't think she ever will; not everyone can spend New Year's Eve playing bingo.

I've always considered myself a woman of sharp intellect, as someone who grasped new concepts quickly, so it's difficult and embarrassing to acknowledge that it took me a long time to accept that this accident had actually happened to me. When I was sufficiently aware of my surroundings, I kept thinking, "This is all a bad dream." I could imagine a six o'clock news story about a young woman who had been the victim of a hit and run accident — and sympathize with her — but I could not imagine it was the story of *my* life. Slowly I realized that my recovery would be a long one, and that I'd have to come to terms with that, however painful. My emotions vacillated between a desperate fear and a raging anger unlike any I had ever known. I was not comfortable with either emotion, nor with the dependency I was forced to accept. After many months and many tears, I learned to embrace these emotions as part of the human spirit, as part of the human condition. I had to allow my vulnerability to show with no excuses. Both were excruciatingly painful lessons, because my pride was bolstered and protected by a strong will, and both had been nurtured over twenty-nine years.

My pride prevented me from accepting that I was confronted with something I couldn't handle alone, and made acknowledging my own vulnerability more than difficult. I wanted desperately to be in control, and I was increasingly frustrated because I knew I wasn't. I took little comfort from the doctors, therapists and friends who assured me that my feelings were normal. "They aren't 'normal' for me," I contended. They only led to self-hate and disgust for my limitations. It seemed that everyone but me — doctors, nurses, insurance companies, my parents — was in control of my life, and I was livid. I lashed out at God especially, continually asking Him what I had done to deserve this punishment, demanding that He explain why He hated me so much. I don't think that I really expected an answer, but I felt He owed me some sort of explanation. I wanted to try and understand what I'd done wrong so that I could "fix it." "Then maybe God would release me from this nightmare," I rationalized. I did not yet understand that there is no rationalization with God, only His Will to be fulfilled. My vulnerability served His purpose, eventually allowing me to approach Him for help, to reach out to Him when I might not have otherwise.

As I said, I acknowledged the reality of my situation very slowly, but as I did the full extent of my injuries became increasingly frightening. I had trouble thinking of words, and putting a simple sentence together was a struggle. I was confined to a wheelchair, my left arm paralyzed and I finally realized there was something very wrong with my eyesight. I wasn't blind; I could see light and shapes roughly, but I couldn't see clearly at all, and I couldn't distinguish between different colors anymore. My blurry vision filled me with fear, but I consoled myself, thinking, "Surely this is only temporary; surely my eyesight will return." The first doctor I asked, Dr. Diamond, who had treated me since the accident, explained that clotting in the four arteries of my neck had almost completely shut off the blood and oxygen supply to my brain, damaging the visual control center. I still took Cumiden, a blood-thinning medication prescribed for me in December, and my doctors predicted I'd take it for the rest of my life. With the exception of a broken leg, all my injuries were brain-related; they affected my sensory and motor functions, my short-term and working memory, my spatial and perceptual capacities, and, worst of all, my vision. My medical records and CAT scans outlined damage to both the left and right occipital lobes of my brain as well as to the right parietal lobe. At the time, his explanation meant very little; I concentrated solely on "How do we fix this? What do I do?" The answer I heard over and over again frightened me more than the threat of blindness: Doctors and therapists alike said, "Time, Joan. Only time will reveal the extent of your recovery." I was not a person who waited for change; I made it, and I couldn't imagine just passively waiting for recovery.

For the most part, my rehabilitation initially centered on adaptation to my residual handicaps through Physical and Occupational Therapy, Neuropsychology, and Speech and Language Therapy rather than on recovering the functions I'd lost in the visual, sensory and spatial components of my brain, as well as some cognitive areas.

God had blessed me with much drive and stamina, and I had achieved many successes through diligence. "You're only as good as your last accomplishment," I always reminded myself and my family. My failures were only greater incentives, pushing me harder to succeed the next time. I believed that drive coupled with determination always brought success. It was only natural that I would apply this formula to my rehabilitation and expect the same results. For the first time in my life, I confronted the reality that all the effort on my part, all the long hours I might devote to my therapy, could not guarantee what I so desperately desired. There were no guarantees that I would walk unaided again, no guarantees the feeling would return to my left hand, and no guarantees I'd ever regain my eyesight or reach the intellectual level I'd attained prior to the accident. All harsh realities to accept individually, and nearly impossible to accept as a package.

I was angry with myself, and I was very angry with God. How could He allow this to happen to me? Why did He hate me so much? Whatever had I done to deserve this? Such questions ran continuously through my mind and often occupied the greater part of my day. Then eventually the rage would flare, and I'd explode: "You knew exactly what to take, didn't you, Lord? You knew exactly how to defeat me! I could've awakened from this horrible accident without an arm or a leg, confined to a wheelchair for the rest of my life, and somehow, I know I would find the strength to go on. But you took my eyesight, and with it, my confidence, my independence, my career — everything I had worked so hard for over the years. How could you let this happen to me?"

I confronted God daily with my rage. I was too engrossed in my own anger and pain to reach out to Him or others and ask for their help in a non-demanding way. I kept thinking, "My eyesight, my arm, and my ability to walk are my birthrights, and I want them back! This isn't my fault."

Since God seemed to give no sign that He heard my demands, I decided that once again I'd rely on my own initiative and hard work to recover. God obviously didn't need another person bothering Him on a daily basis — I was sure He had enough of those — and He didn't seem to be responding anyway. I set out, instead, to resolve my handicaps in my own way. I'd never shied away from hard work before, and I didn't intend to now. I still believed God was out there, most definitely, but I also firmly believed that "God helps those who help themselves." I adopted this same philosophy in my therapy. I felt getting through this ordeal was solely my responsibility. With my will and stubbornness, I was determined to find my own way.

Based on my injuries, a rehabilitation program was designed to address my physical and cognitive deficits. As an in-patient, my exercises consisted of Physical Therapy (PT), Occupational Therapy (OT), Communication Skills (CS), Psychology, Recreation Therapy, and Neuropsychology. I realized I was starting a new life — a life centered around rehabilitation, therapists and doctors for quite some time; a life not controlled by me; a life I grew to hate and fear. What I had been and the life I had known were gone, and it was a long time before I could lay claim to that person I had once been.

My day began when a nurse entered my room to help me out of bed and into my wheelchair, then pushed me to a sink in the room, where I washed my face and brushed my teeth. She then helped me dress, assisted me in brushing my hair, and tied my tennis shoes. My left arm, damaged by the stroke, was entirely useless, and it hung motionless at my side. I was completely dependent for all my basic needs. Once dressed and strapped into my wheelchair (to prevent me from sliding out), I ate breakfast in my room. A nurse assisted me, because I couldn't easily identify the food or objects on my plate. After breakfast, a volunteer wheeled me to my first therapy.

My daily schedule went something like this:

9:00 a.m.	Occupational Therapy
10:00 a.m.	Neuropsychology
11:00 a.m.	Communication skills.
11:30 a.m.	Lunch with OT therapist
2:15 p.m.	Physical Therapy
3:15 p.m.	Recreation

During my first session with my neuropsychology therapist, we discussed methods to retrain my memory. We also set up a log book, in which each therapist, and often my parents, recorded the exercises and events of each day. With this book, I had a record of my progress and a way to review the events of the day, thus further exercising my memory.

At the bottom of this first page in my notebook, my OT therapist made a note: "Plate guard is on bureau to use during meals over the weekend." The plate guard was an adaptive device which assisted me in identifying and containing the food on my plate and compensated for my visual and left hand impairments. It helped me make my first move toward feeding myself.

Often, a nurse or therapist would note in my records, "Joan makes minimal attempts to verbalize." I was capable of responding to the people around me, but in most cases, I had no desire to do so. Although I could form words clearly, I put them together only slowly and hesitantly. I sat in my wheelchair, speaking only when pressed, using short, deliberate sentences. Often I felt as if I knew what I wanted to say, but I couldn't get the words out in the necessary order, couldn't get my point across — and often didn't care enough to work at it.

I knew I wasn't the most outgoing or enthusiastic patient. I felt trapped in a cloud of blurry images and forgetfulness, and I was so distraught and angry that I couldn't bring myself to pretend, even for a moment, that I was happy that I had survived the accident. Sometimes I cried out to God, "Why didn't You just let me die? This is too hard, Lord. This cross is too heavy. You picked the wrong person for this one."

I am ashamed of these words now, and I debated over including them here. But to omit them is to deny my own feelings as well as the pain I gave my parents. They could only stand by helplessly, watching their daughter's despair. I did not feel alive; I merely went through the motions, tried to get through each day — often a task that seemed impossible. I told my parents that I couldn't wait to get "another day over with," and that my favorite time was finally crawling into my bed at night. And this is ironic too, because one of the few things I kept to myself was my hatred for that hospital bed in Harmarville, with its bars on the side, and the "call" button I pushed when I needed a bed-pan. Some memories never leave me.

I suppose I had to hit bottom before I could begin the long and difficult climb back up. For a while, I actually gave up control of my life, vacillating between periods of rage and despair and periods of complete, quiet indifference. Often I was so emotionally drained that I submitted silently to whatever activities or exercises the doctors and therapists chose. The thought of docilely relinquishing such control to other people was once unthinkable to me, and it frightens me even now to realize I did just that. I was ashamed because I couldn't meet my own needs without asking for assistance, and this shame drove me deeper into despair. Caught between self-pity and self-hate daily, I could not accept this floundering, dependent person, a woman confined to a wheelchair, her mind as blurry as her vision. The confident, strong woman who once motivated all the people around her found it increasingly difficult to motivate herself. "Where is that woman who never quit on herself, or allowed others to quit? Where is that go-getter, that over-achiever, who wowed them at IBM?" I cried myself to sleep each night, asking these questions. I was so wrapped in my own pain and struggle that I couldn't bear to reach out to others. "Why should others see my pain? They have their own troubles, and they certainly don't need to see mine," I argued. I tried to protect them from what I had become physically as well as the chaotic emotions I felt. I didn't want anyone to feel I must be accepted as I was. More than that, I tried to protect myself: If I couldn't accept who I was, how could they? My fears were confirmed by the evident discomfort and awkwardness I read and felt in the manners of several visitors, some of them people who professed to love me. On the few occasions when I felt pressured or obligated to see certain friends, we were both relieved when the visit ended. They must have felt that they too were dealing with someone they didn't know. It was difficult, I am sure, to tell me that I "looked terrific," or exclaim on what great progress I'd made. It was even more difficult to sit in that wheelchair, aware of their scrutiny, and feel compelled to say I was still the same person, and that I still felt the same toward them and toward myself. This was one of the few times in my life when I couldn't argue well enough to convince myself or others. Armed with the painful memories of those few encounters, I retreated further from all the people around me. That many others could not accept me as I was became my excuse to hide. Only my parents seemed to accept me — but they "had to," I told myself. I am ashamed of how often I took them for granted, and how much my words must have hurt them, especially when I consider the pain they'd already gone through. But in my rages I cared for no one's feelings but my own. We were all frightened; we were all angry; we were all aware of my increasing isolation.

I worked hard to hide my rages from people outside my family — my emotions were too personal and too incriminating, and I was afraid I couldn't contain them. I never lashed out at anyone physically, but I remember banging my head against a door, crying uncontrollably, "I just want my eyesight back. I just want my eyesight." It didn't seem to matter whether I yelled or just cried softly. God just didn't seem to hear me or to care. I felt so damned alone; nobody understood what I was going through, how petrified I was of not seeing, how frightened of being dependent for life. "I don't know how to be dependent," I cried, "What am I supposed to do? Ask somebody to marry me? Nobody wants damaged goods, Lord. I am not going to inflict myself on anyone." On this matter, my mind was made up; a miracle would hardly change it, as many who knew me confirmed. God knew this about me, too, and I suppose He knew He had one tough nut to crack. My pride and my will were my greatest handicaps in the many months ahead. I progressed in my various therapies, but my recovery was painfully slow.

The doctors' reports regarding my eyesight were anything but encouraging. I saw Dr. Kennerdell in February of 1987, for a full neuro-ophthalmic examination.

In a later deposition, Dr. Kennerdell noted that my visual acuity, in terms of the 20/20 scale, was 2200- in the right eye and 2400 in the left. This meant, roughly, that I saw at 20 feet what an average person saw at 200 feet. Imagine a hockey rink. Put an eye chart at one end, and yourself at the other. Now try to read it. That's what my vision was like when I tried to read a chart 20 feet away from me. I still couldn't see colors, I had blind spots, and my visual field — the range of area I could see — was limited.

My neuro-opthamologist said flatly, "Well, you're legally blind, but you're young, and you'll adjust." I thought, "Legally blind? What had I been before the accident — illegally sighted?" As if those words weren't devastating enough, his assistant put the final nail in the coffin. After the examination, I told him about the positions I'd held at IBM, and how I'd traveled around the world. I commented that I certainly was anxious to resume my career, once I was well again. The man simply shook his head and walked out of the room. I was hurt, and I didn't immediately register that his body language and his dismissal of the subject were a way of saying that I would not return to work. Again I fought to hold my emotions in check, and I tried to tell the neuro-opthamologist about some research I'd done which concerned the possibility of retraining undamaged parts of the brain to take over for damaged areas. I told him of an article (given to me by a woman whose daughter was also a patient at Harmarville) which told of a young girl whose visual cortex was almost completely destroyed as a result of anoxic brain injury. Through selected therapies administered by a neuropsychologist, the girl regained her eyesight and returned to school. "Is this possible?" I asked, desperately looking for hope. Again, he dismissed me, this time with a wave of his hand. "They do quirky things" — referring I suppose, to neuropsychologists.

As for other parts of the brain taking over for damaged parts, he commented quite matter-of-factly: "We don't see recovery in that area [the occipital lobes] of the brain." The back tip of my brain was damaged in the upper section, which is where the vision center is located. During the accident, my car had been hit with such force that I suffered whiplash so severe that my brain was battered against the back of my skull and bruised. In addition, I had lost most of the blood circulation to that part of the brain, which caused even more tissue damage.

Dr. Kennerdell told me that I had, in effect, lost the brain tissue that tells the eyes to see, and he totally dismissed the idea of retraining my existing visual capacity. Instead he recommended adaptive devices, such as telescopic lenses and magnification tools, which might make the best of my remaining sight.

My parents and I left his office in a daze, emotionally and physically drained, and went to a coffee shop. I remember thinking, "We should really be going to a bar." As we sat there, going over the doctor's pronouncement, I tried to bolster my courage by recalling the predictions doctors made in those initial weeks after my accident, many of which I had already proved false. A person with two clotted neck arteries did not survive, but I survived clots in all four of my neck arteries. My broken leg was healing well. There were no precedents; my injury and my survival were a first. Perhaps my recovery would be too.

That week, in Occupational Therapy, I practiced standing, then pivoting to sit in my wheelchair. I also took a verbal I.Q. test and a functional memory test. The latter confirmed my doctors' diagnosis, that I could mentally store information much more easily than I could retrieve it, particularly when dealing with new information. This was one reason forming sentences was initially so difficult for me.

Through the next few weeks I practiced standing and turning, all the while favoring my right leg, and I practiced hopping to prepare for the crutches I'd eventually use. On January 12, 1987, almost five weeks after the accident, I had an appointment with Dr. Reimer (my orthopedic surgeon) who told me that my leg was healing nicely, but that it was still too weak to bear my full weight. The next day, I practiced using a walker; with it I traveled 400 feet.

I was alive, and slowly I was making progress. But instead of being glad I had survived, I remained despondent. How could I forget about my eyesight? The reality of blindness was always there, from the time I awoke in the morning until I fell asleep at night. At times this cross seemed impossible to carry. But somehow I found the strength to carry it for another day. Although I didn't realize it at the time, God heard my prayers and saw my despondency, and He responded in His own way and in His own time. I can look back, now, and understand that I needed to "let go, and let God." But again, I learned this lesson very slowly.

Part of my Occupational Therapy centered on improving my motor skills and developing my spatial sense. As an exercise, I endlessly folded towels, each one stenciled with "HARMARVILLE" in black letters. I felt utterly humiliated; I was working at menial tasks — and often failing at them. Because I couldn't see or imagine the spatial dimensions of the towel, merely matching the corners as I folded them took all my effort and concentration. I thought of the high-flying career woman I had been and the rewards and achievements I'd attained. To struggle at a trivial task, when I well remembered the respect I'd once earned with my ability to create and produce, was a devastating blow to my pride and my self-confidence. "If I can't fold a towel properly, how can I ever go back to work?" I thought constantly, and the idea deepened my shame.

I also worked extensively at strengthening my left arm, and at using my left hand to stabilize objects. Since the stroke, I had very little sensation in it, and I had to relearn where, and in what direction, to move my fingers if I wanted to grip anything. In my log book, the Occupational Therapist wrote, "Joan questioned whether the intent of the exercises was to make her ambidextrous. I replied that the exercise was to gain back normal use of hand and arm." I wanted to heal, not adapt to, my injuries, and I wanted my therapeutic exercises designed toward that goal.

I kept working on my memory to improve my recall. In some ways, I had to learn a sense of logic and ordering, the lessons we learn as children almost unknowingly, all over again. I learned to associate my therapists' names with their area through alphabetical similarities when possible — for example, Lori = Language. I also practiced memorizing and categorizing information. We often played a game similar to the $20,000 Pyramid. I, like other brain-injured people, developed my own techniques as well. Again, the triviality and simplicity of these exercises was glaringly apparent to me. My difficulty in performing simple, repetitive tasks only symbolized the extent of my injury, particularly with my working memory.

I needed to believe there was some type of therapy out there that could heal me. My faith seemed to take me only so far; I knew I was looking for a miracle, and as I tried to justify my search for it, I became even more angry with myself and with God; to believe in miracles, to ask for one, was to admit helplessness, something I had never felt in my life.

I did my best, with people other than my family, to give the impression of being in control. I identified with a commercial that played frequently around that time. It advertised hair-coloring, and at its close actress Linda Evans said, "I don't intend to age gracefully; I intend to fight it every step of the way." I told my doctor that "I didn't intend to just accept my eyesight like this; I intended to fight it every step of the way." I think how strong those words must have sounded, and I know the great fear they tried to hide.

I had always believed in a loving God Who wanted us whole and well, and even in my despair and rage, I refused to believe that God would bring me this far only to let me down. Still, it took time for me to firmly believe that my life was spared for a reason, that a Higher Power had determined that I still had more work in this world to do. While I can state those words with firm conviction now, there were many times during my rehabilitation, when I resorted to asking, once again, whether God heard me at all.

I had much to learn about God, about others, and about dealing with my handicaps. I couldn't let go of the fact that I was still here — that I had survived a catastrophic and unique injury despite the doctors' offer of little hope. "Why had I survived?" I asked myself and God, over and over again. The only answer I could imagine was that God decided that my number wasn't up on Interstate 80, that I still had more work in this world to do, but what sort of work? I had no ready answer for that question. It was many months before I recognized the plan laid out for me. In the meantime, I had many trials to confront and much to learn about the source of inner strength.

In the meantime, I worked on in my therapy, grinding out each day, sometimes full of determination, ready to "show" all around me, and God too, that I would recover through sheer force of will, and sometimes only participating because there seemed nothing else left to me. Slowly, my ability to speak and carry on a conversation improved. Struggling to separate "light" colors from "dark" ones, I chose tiles to make a trivet in Occupational Therapy. I worked on strengthening my good left leg, learning to balance and hop, preparing to move from the walker to crutches. In Physical Therapy, I lay across a large rubber ball, relearning my sense of balance and how to maintain it. One of the longest and most frustrating lessons was learning again to dress myself. The simple act of pulling on a sweat shirt was beyond me.

There were some small triumphs, times when I felt sure that I would recover. One day, I sat in my wheel chair in the speech therapist's office. She was called out, and as I sat waiting for her, I stared at the wall behind her desk. Often I tried to see the things around me, straining my eyes to make out objects, to identify things just out of my reach, but that day I only sat and looked ahead. Slowly I realized that I could see something that I hadn't seen in a long while. There was a colored blur on the wall, and I remember thinking, "Lavender. That's lavender." When Lori returned, I said, "Look, Lori. Is that color behind you lavender?"

She twisted around in her chair. "Why, yes, it is," she said. "It's a poster, and the background is lavender."

Just like that, I could see colors — and name some of them — again. That night, as I lay in my bed, my good right hand feeling the cool metal guards on the sides, I was sure if I waited long enough, worked hard enough, I'd get it all back.

On January 9, 1987, my vision was retested by a neuropsychologist and a therapist. They examined my color vision, my hand-eye coordination, object/face recognition, and peripheral vision. There were also tests in word problem-solving, with questions that began "What would you do if...." and tests that examined my ability to follow commands using both the right and left limbs. I had improved in all areas except my vision.

The doctors, the therapists, and some friends and family members began talking to me about accepting and learning to deal with my handicaps. I resisted their efforts to move me towards acceptance, focusing on one goal instead: the restoration of my eyesight. Without it, I couldn't imagine much promise for my future, only a life of dependency. I was petrified. I knew I had to make some adaptations — if only temporarily — to deal as a legally blind person in a sighted world, even though I resented the push to do so. I would not, however, give up hope of finally recovering my vision. That thought was firmly fixed in my mind, and I was determined to prove all the doctors and therapists wrong. I actively sought reading material on the brain, asking my parents to read it to me, and I learned that the brain had an amazing capacity to heal and recover from injury. I clung to the fact that no one really knew how a trillion neurons within the brain reacted or recovered. I remember thinking, as my mother read information to me, that maybe the brain was where the soul resides. The brain, after all, was what made each of us different and unique individuals. As much as the medical field professed to know about the brain in 1987, there was still more that they didn't know about its workings. I saw that unknown as my "ace," my hope, in the difficult months ahead. I saw it as my avenue to actively work at getting back the capacities I had lost. I consoled myself and my parents by reminding them that I'd worked for a company that produced the most incredible computers in the information-processing industry, yet IBM couldn't begin to produce a computer that replicated the intricate and numerous functions normally regulated and controlled by the human brain.

Whenever I spoke of regaining my eyesight to doctors and therapists, I felt the tension level increase in the room, and felt rather than saw the quiet shaking of heads. They (correctly) interpreted my search for full recovery as a refusal to accept their reality. Despite the progress I was making verbally and mentally, they believed I'd never recover my eyesight as it had been, nor my cognitive and sensory capacities. I chose to believe that I would recover my lost capacities, particularly, my vision. I kept a mental list of the limitations my doctors predicted, and I watched their surprise when their prognoses did not come to fruition.

On January 17th, I went home for the first time on a weekend pass. This was an emotional and psychological turning point, for it both marked my improved physical condition and helped me come to terms with the reality of my accident. After almost two solid months of institutionalization, experiencing life only from a wheelchair and a hospital bed in a place that was foreign to me, I was finally going to my parents' home. This trip also forced me to acknowledge that I needed institutionalization. I could leave Harmarville for a restricted amount of time, but I must return, and I couldn't leave without a doctor's written permission. My insurance company stipulated that I couldn't leave for more than 48 hours, or they would cancel my status as an inpatient and discontinue payments toward my bills. Once again, doctors and insurance companies set limits on my life.

I can remember vividly my nervous anticipation about making that first trip home. I was excited, but I was afraid of reaching home only to find that my dog, Peanut, had not survived this horrible accident. My parents knew I was anxious about him, and they repeatedly tried to reassure me that he had survived. They even described the doctor at Clarion Hospital who had taken Peanut home with her until my father and Michael claimed him. As much as I wanted to believe them, I couldn't until I saw him for myself. I knew it would be difficult for me to actually "see" Peanut, but I hoped other clues would help me recognize him. Would he come when I called? Would he know me, even if I could not recognize him? Part of my worry sprang from my own memory lapses; I could neither fix in my mind that he was alive or assure myself that I would know him if I saw him.

In a flurry of nerves and questions, I made that first trip home. My father bumped me up the walkway in my wheelchair, to the front door of our house. My mother went ahead to open the front door while I sat impatiently waiting. Finally, I was inside the front hallway, and this small cream-colored ball of fur jumped up excitedly and licked my face repeatedly. From what I could see, it certainly looked and acted like Peanut, and he seemed to recognize me, but I still couldn't be sure. I kept looking at him, wondering if this was a replacement my parents had bought.

They teased me, amused that I thought they might try to fool me with a new dog. "You should know he's irreplaceable, Joanie, just like his owner," they said.

Peanut and I spent the entire time I was home getting reacquainted, and we had a wonderful time. It was good to laugh again, and to be safe and warm within my parents' home with a fire burning in the fireplace. This was the home I remembered, even if I couldn't see it too well. I felt warm and safe, something I hadn't felt in a very long time. Sleeping in my own room, in my own bed, without waking to the loud voices of other people in pain, was a gift I was grateful for. Being home with my parents and my dog, if only for a short while, was the best therapy I could have had, and knowing I would return each following weekend helped lessen the pain of knowing I was only home for a short while.

Yet the pleasure of being home didn't wipe out the changes the accident had made in our lives, and it didn't alleviate my helplessness and my resentment. It was hard to let my parents care for me as if I was a small child. With my mother, I was more vocal, often venting my frustration on her. At 30, I was incapable of the smallest tasks, and I was humiliated by my dependence on her.

Just being out in the world again, trying again the smallest errands and activities, struck chords in me that I could not recognize or control. Saturday evening my father added a note to my log book:

> *While riding on the Parkway into town for a hair appointment, Joan suddenly exclaimed, "Where do I go? Where do I go?" I asked her what she meant. Joan said that she remembered being in a car, and suddenly, "there was nowhere to go." I did not push it beyond that. In her accident, she was bumped off the road as she was about to pass a truck. She lost control of her car, and spun out onto the highway, facing an on-coming 18-wheeler which hit her head-on. This seemed to be a flashback to the accident, the first and the only brief recollection she has had of it.*

CHAPTER FOUR

PROGRESS

ON MONDAYS I RETURNED TO HARMARVILLE, determined to recover the person I was. That day in therapy, I worked on guiding my stroke-damaged left hand with my right hand, prompting it to grasp objects. I traced figures with two fingers, retraining my mind to recognize geometric shapes and a few letters. I could recognize four- and six-sided figures visually, and a few others were familiar after I followed the shape with my right hand. I told my neuropsychology therapist that this was all less "like a dream," and more like my life, or what was left of it.

My talk with her was one more sign, to me as well as the people around me, that I was beginning to understand and accept the reality of my situation. Throughout the months of my rehabilitation, I came to acknowledge a strength which grew within me; it presented itself during my most difficult moments, and it encouraged me to get out of bed and proceed with my therapies each day, pushing my resentment to the back of my mind long enough to get through another day. "I have to approach my therapies as a job," I coached myself. "This is my job, now," I told my parents, and I worked hard at it, especially those therapies that were designed to help me become self-sufficient again.

Even my weekend trips home, short moves away from the support system at Harmarville, presented problems. There were several discussions between my family and my therapists about ways I might shower while I was at home. I was still confined to a wheelchair, and showering at

Harmarville wasn't too much of a problem, because I could be wheeled directly into the shower stall. But my parents' home, with its regular bathrooms and narrow doorways, didn't allow for the same method. Finally we devised a means for me to shower while sitting in a chair. After I crawled on my backside up the hallway stairs to the shower in my parents' bedroom, my mother assisted me in sitting in a plastic chair placed in the shower stall. Then I could shower alone. Over the weeks, I became more proficient at the transfers, but not more comfortable with accepting the assistance I needed for such a simple task. Then too, for whatever reason, the surgery scars on my hip and right knee were more apparent to me in my parents' shower. I could discern just where the staples had been placed on my right knee and hip. Even as I ran my hand over them, it seemed incredible that my leg was so badly broken. In one meeting, I asked the surgeon, Dr. Reimer, whether I would set off alarms at airport security checks. I imagined myself traveling again for IBM, and the problems my leg might cause, setting off alarms in international airports all over the world. He replied that he didn't think so. Even after such concrete discussions, I found it hard to believe there were pins and a rod in my leg, and hard to remember that I must be very careful not to put my full weight on it. It was easier to imagine that I would return to IBM, but that, of course, remained to be seen.

My Occupational Therapist also developed a specific, step-by-step set of instructions to direct me in putting on my sweatshirt. This was my first move toward dressing alone. Every morning I slowly went through these steps, aided by a therapist or by my mother:

Step 1.   Lay sweatshirt on Joan's lap, so that back is face up, waistband by waist, collar by feet, left arm on left side, right arm on right side.

Step 2.   Joan verbally identifies above mentioned parts as she feels where they are.

Step 3.   Joan verbally goes through the steps of putting sweatshirt on.

Step 4.   Left arm, hand fisted, goes through left sleeve, push up past elbow.
Step 5.   Right arm goes through waistband up through right sleeve.
Step 6.   Head goes through waistband, and then collar.

At Harmarville, this assistance was considered part of my "ADL's," or Activities of Daily Living therapy. Either way, the whole process was humiliating. I resented such specific directions and assistance, but I grudgingly admitted that I did need that supervision. To me, my limited eyesight was my greatest deterrent; I was sure it prevented me from dressing readily and independently. "If only I could see," I thought, "then dressing wouldn't be a problem."

But, as I learned in the following weeks, it was actually the combination of all my brain injuries that made dressing such a difficult task. It was almost impossible, it seemed, to discern where objects were in space, or in relation to my body. The stroke left me with only minimal feeling in my left arm, and this made pushing my left arm through its sleeve an almost fruitless effort. My days started with my dressing battle, and my success at that struggle determined my attitude and productivity for the rest of the day. I was not used to feeling so defeated.

Before the accident, I was someone who looked forward to each day, always anxious to get started. Now I dreaded each day merely because it began with dressing. An employee of mine wrote me a letter during those initial weeks of my recovery, and my mother read it to me. He wrote, "I'll never forget the way you used to come rushing up the steps and into your office in the morning. You actually looked happy to be there." On hearing this comment, I remember smiling and then saying, very seriously, "they really didn't understand me, did they? I really WAS glad to be there!" I loved working, and I especially loved managing a department, headaches and all. I thrived on it.

"Will it ever be that way, again, Mom?" I asked her. She simply hugged me. I knew she was hurting, too.

That same week I practiced opening a milk carton, using my right hand as a guide. I also folded more Harmarville towels. For me, this therapy continued to be an exercise in humiliation. I did it without complaint, all the while seething inside. I thought of all the challenging managerial decisions and tasks I was once responsible for, and this job felt like a slap in the face.

Dressing continued to be both a physical and an emotional battle for me. The anger I felt because I couldn't dress myself without supervision seemed insurmountable. I shed many, many tears at home over the weekends. I was too angry and too proud to let those at Harmarville see my tears of frustration, but I saved each one to shed at home, where I felt protected and known by my family. I couldn't totally mask my frustration, and, sensing it, my OT therapist tried to decrease the tension by conducting extra practice sessions with me, in the privacy of the OT clinic bathroom. We focused on correctly slipping on my sweatshirt. I knew only practice would help me overcome this seemingly impossible task, and I was determined to master it.

I progressed slowly in my therapies — too slowly to take much satisfaction from them — but I consoled myself by thinking that the people at Harmarville had much to learn about Joan Ulicny. "They don't know what my talents are, and what I'm capable of," I thought. I had so much to learn about myself, and about the source of inner strength.

While I did my best to maintain some outward appearance of calm, inside I was an emotional tangle of knots and unceasing questions to God. "What have I done to deserve this?" I asked Him repeatedly. "Why have You forgotten me?" I cringed inwardly at this last question, even as it rose up in my mind, because God and I both knew that for many years I acted as though I had forgotten Him, yet my life had been spared. "What could you possibly want from me that justified sparing my life?" I had no idea. Even in the infant stages of my ability to recognize that I was still alive only by the grace of God, I was too afraid to imagine what the reason might be. Instead of listening and searching, I rationalized, creating my own answer: Obviously, I had done something terribly wrong to deserve this. I saw my situation as punishment for neglecting God, for the many years of lip-service I had paid Him. I had much to learn about how God works, and about His infinite mercy. He continued to be patient with me, even when I was far from being patient with Him. Slowly I began to recover some of my strength and mobility.

On Saturday, January 24, I was at my parents', sitting in their family room, lifting weights to exercise the left side of my body. I had just finished a set of leg lifts, using 2½ pound ankle weights. My father had been "coaching" me; he kept count as I raised my legs, and also as I struggled to lift my hands over my head, guiding my clumsy left hand by grasping it with my right. After the tenth arm stretch, I rested, sitting with my back against the couch. The television was on, and my father sat in a chair across from me. I absently moved both my hands, because my therapist had told me to keep working the left one, to keep trying to flex and strengthen it. Then I realized my father was leaning forward, watching me attentively. I looked at my left hand, squinting to make it out against the blue rug. Still I could feel nothing, but it looked curled, fingers in against the palm. I held it up close to my eyes, then showed it to my father again, and we both realized I was clenching it, making a fist, for the first time since the accident. After eight weeks, I could open and close my hand. He was so excited; he called my mother, and they both watched as I flexed it again. I couldn't even pretend to share their happiness; it was such a small thing, and so far from the progress I wanted to make.

On Monday, I started learning my way around the treatment areas at Harmarville. I worked with my neuropsychologist, creating a mental map of the hallways, and she wrote down the memory cues that seemed to work best for me in my journal so I could review them:

(1)   Immediately outside of Unit Four, where Joan's room is located, is the patient library and PT room.

(2)   Pass secretary, turn right. Three doors up on right is the neuropsychology group. Note the blue wall with panels. CS is the seventh door on right. Across the hall is hand therapy.

With these directions, I started developing a sense of the space around me, and I imagined negotiating my way through my surroundings, working toward a time when I needn't wait for a volunteer aid to wheel me from therapy to therapy.

At that time, I felt completely isolated. With my right leg still weak, and my left leg and arm stiff and almost useless from the stroke, I couldn't move my wheelchair alone for any distance at all. If the aid responsible for transporting me was late (and they often were), I could only wait — and I hated waiting. For me, it only underlined my helplessness and the length of time between me and complete recovery.

One day I sat in my wheel chair, waiting once again, and fuming. I was sure I was late for Physical Therapy, but I couldn't move myself, and I wasn't even sure of the time. Across the room, I could just make out a roundish, silver platter on the wall. From where I sat, it looked like the wide metal clocks in every room of my old Catholic grade school. I remembered the firm black numbers, comfortingly clear and unambiguous on a white face, and the large black hands — surely I could read *that*. I could figure out what time it was, and then I'd tell the aid how late she was! Slowly, using my right hand on each runner, I wrestled my wheel chair across the room, directly under the clock. I stared at it, squinting and concentrating, feeling if I could only focus a little more, the numbers would jump into focus. Soon I sensed someone standing behind me. Jim, one of the nurses working that day, stood for a moment, then asked me, offhandedly, "What're you doing, Joan?" It was clear what I was doing! Suddenly I was angry again, furious with him for implying that I was wasting my time trying to see. "Jim — just let me alone. I know if I work at this, I can read this clock. I want to know what time it is." I turned back to the wall. He stood for a moment more, then said gently, "Well, it's going to be difficult. Because that's a fire alarm on the wall." Shocked, I looked down. I knew immediately he was right. There were, of course, no numbers at all on the smooth, silver disk. I struggled not to cry. "Of course," I said. Then he walked off, too compassionate to say anything else. Again, I was devastated. I don't know what kept me from going back to my room and crying the rest of the day — except that same stubbornness that insisted I could read a nonexistant clock.

But that same tenacity did serve me in other ways. On January 26, my physical therapist made a note in my journal: "Joan discussed with therapist why it was necessary for her to be strapped into her wheelchair. Therapist could give no good reason." This was significant; it demonstrated my ability to question "procedure." However slowly, my intellect was beginning to reveal itself. Less than two months after my accident, I was challenging an accepted policy, asking why I must be strapped into my wheelchair when my awareness and balance had improved considerably. I had redeveloped the mental capacity necessary to question outright things I might have docilely accepted earlier.

Although I could now clench my left hand, I still couldn't feel pressure, and this interfered with my grip on the handle, so I couldn't use two crutches. Instead, I practiced hopping on my left leg, training myself to move on it and on one crutch held in my right hand. So often my injuries seemed to compound each other. Sometimes I felt as if every part of my body was conspiring against me. I practiced hopping and did exercises with 7½ pound weights, preparing myself for the time when I could trade my wheelchair and walker for a crutch which would substitute for my right leg. The surgeon hadn't yet allowed me to try my full weight on it. My therapist tested and built up the right arm of one crutch. She explained that as I worked with them, we'd adjust the fit as my strength and abilities changed.

Through the following difficult months I came to understand that God gave crosses as a sign of His love, and that he used them to call a person back to Him. It was many months before I embraced my Cross with a love equal to that with which it was given. The road to acceptance was a long and difficult journey, made more hurtful by my own pride and lack of faith. My own will, along with the deep conviction that I must handle my recovery myself, kept getting in the way. To ask God for a miracle at this point, with regard to my eyesight, never occurred to me; asking for God's help was admitting total helplessness, and that I couldn't do.

I was very much a product of the eighties. Always using and refining my skills and my talents, I believed I could rely only on them for success in a competitive world. "Never settle," was my attitude, "always strive to be better. No one is going to do it for you." That was my philosophy, and there was little, if any, room for helplessness or for God. I stood firm in this conviction for many years before my accident, and I was not likely to abandon it in the trials I saw ahead of me. But all the while my Creator stood by patiently, waiting for my anger and my pride to subside. His wait would be a long one; I marvel at His patience. I, on the other hand, was too impatient to wait for His assistance. "I want my eyesight, and I want it now! It's my birthright. How dare you take it away from me?" I raged. My feelings were barriers He had to break down before I could let Him help me, and my conversion was a painful and slow process. I realize now that it could be no other way. As the birth of a baby is preceded by physical pain, my rebirth into a new life, where God was finally reinstated to His rightful place at the center of it, was painful too. Taking that step meant denying myself, taking up my cross, and following Him. That awareness, however, was not possible for me in 1987. I was too wrapped up in my own pain to see God's Hand in anything. Instead, I chose to overcome my handicaps by applying myself even more diligently to my therapies.

In small ways, I learned to work with my limitations, always with self-reliance and with ultimate full recovery as my goal. For showers, I started using a wash mitt on my stiff left hand. I couldn't hold a regular wash cloth with it, but I could use my right hand to pull the mitt down over my left, where it stayed in place as I washed. I made use of a "rocker" knife that allowed me to cut my food, using my right hand only. I stuck a piece of velcro on the back of my right shoe, so I could distinguish between it and the left one. My therapists attached velcro to the back of my sweatshirts and the front of my sweat pants, to help me orient the clothing to my body more quickly. Despite my determination to heal my injuries, rather than merely accepting and adapting to them, I did adapt in little ways. I could not deny the assistance provided to me by the velcro placed on my clothes and shoes, but this last innovation stung my pride each time I depended on it, and I was determined to grow beyond it.

I advanced slowly from the wheelchair to hopping on one crutch, and then to using my right leg for very short periods. Somehow I never doubted that someday I would walk unaided. I can vividly remember closing the door to my room at Harmarville to practice walking with no assistance. I had no fear, regardless of the warnings that my right leg was very fragile and weak. "I'll prove them all wrong," I thought determinedly. Again, I was so quick to take credit for achievements to come, refusing to acknowledge the Hand of the One Who had brought me this far. I had yet to learn to give credit where it is due.

In therapy I practiced recognizing objects by touch, concentrating on my right hand at first. My sense of space and my sense of knowing the world improved slowly. I practiced hopping with my "custom-fitted" crutch. By the end of January I could hop 500 feet and could almost navigate the wide, low stairs at Harmarville alone.

In occupational therapy, I graduated from folding towels to putting pillow cases on pillows, a task exasperating enough to reduce me to tears. Without proper cuing from the therapist, my visual, perceptual and spatial deficits combined to make this an impossible task. Just as I had trouble orienting my clothing to my body, I could not correctly orient the pillow to the pillowcase without her help. My left hand was totally useless in this task, just as it was in the towel-folding exercise. "What an absolute mess I am," I berated myself, inwardly. "Only a shell of what I once was."

Then the rage would return, and I'd pound my fist on the top of the tray attached to my wheelchair, proclaiming to my parents that I would not allow doctors and therapists to dictate my life. I thought that they had drawn their own conclusions about my ability to achieve full recovery, and it seemed they saw only a negative and limited future. Doctors and therapists alike seemed to be talking about adaptation, not resolution, of my handicaps.

I wanted nothing to do with adaptation. I only wanted to know how I could go about regaining what I had lost. In turn, they insisted that I needed to move toward accepting my handicaps. I was told to make use of all the adaptive devices available, because these would make dealing with my residual handicaps easier. "Easier for whom?" I thought, "my therapists or me?" I never embraced the adaptive strategies my therapists or doctors recommended, and I bristled at suggestions that I should do so.

I particularly had no intention of just accepting and adapting to eyesight "like this." "If God had meant for me to be blind, legally or otherwise, wouldn't He have taken it all?" I asked myself repeatedly. I believed that He knew I needed my eyesight for whatever work my life had been spared for, and on some unacknowledged level, I was becoming more certain that He did have some specific purpose for me. Somehow, surrounded by skeptics and critics of my defiance, I never stopped believing that I would see clearly once again. Sometimes my own faith did falter, and

I almost allowed myself to accept the "structuralist" point of view — that I would never see again as I once had. Then something would help me escape that despair, and again I'd set my goals on recovering everything I'd lost.

By early February, my perception of colors had improved, and I could write a letter on a word processor to a friend. My therapist commented that the letter showed good organization of thought and working memory. While I could not see the letters on the screen, I knew their placement on the key board. At that time, I didn't dream it possible to attain something greater than what I had lost and sorely mourned. Slowly, however, I was moving toward a vision that allowed me to see things I might never have been able to see prior to my accident.

Thursday, February 5, 1987 was very important to me, because it marked the first visit IBM personnel made to my rehab environment. I was petrified by the thought of this meeting. I was very conscious of my dependency, and I dreaded attending this meeting in a wheelchair, even though my legs were the least of my problems. Although I wished this visit would never occur, as a former IBM manager, I understood its necessity. Almost three months had passed since my accident, and as my employer IBM was certainly entitled to send my manager and personnel manager to visit me to assess my performance ability. I thought they were coming to evaluate how soon — or if — I could return to work; I felt they were coming to judge me, and I couldn't bear to think that my job might not be waiting for me. I was sure that they would take one look at the helpless, drifting creature I'd become and compare her to the woman they had worked with — I made the same comparison every day. I should have realized Chris and Joe came to visit me primarily as friends. Pride is an awful thing, and I am ashamed that I almost allowed it to stand between me and two very special friends. Joe Hines, my personnel manager, was totally blind, the result of a motorcycle accident almost 20 years earlier. If anyone could attempt to understand how I felt, Joe could. With Chris, my second-line manager, the man I reported to directly, I found myself more guarded. Chris was the second-line manager for two other departments as well as mine. These were no small responsibilities, and I felt very guilty that I was not back in New York, assisting him with internal management affairs. My accident had occurred at the worst possible time. The branch I worked for was in the process of transferring from New York to Boulder, Colorado, at the time of my accident. At this crucial time, I was not there to assist in placing my employees in new job assignments, and I felt that no one knew them, no one could settle them in the best jobs but me. I felt I was letting my staff down. Although I put up my best front, talking cheerfully, mentioning that I'd soon "be out of this place" and working again, I was sure they weren't fooled, and deep inside, I wasn't either. Forced to look at my injuries through my old manager's perceptions, I was confronted with their reality. I felt my job, my place in the world, slipping away as I talked with Joe and Chris.

The next day, I returned to my old routine, grimly determined to hold on to my old life. I still practiced hopping, the therapist readily assisting at my left arm. I practiced ascending and descending stairs. By then I needed only minimal assistance to maintain my balance.

That same week, a neuropsychology therapist retested my memory using the Rivermead Test, and noted some improvement. It was still hard for me to store new information and retrieve it; she included more memory strategies, such as rehearsal and visualization in my schedule. In one exercise I listened to three, four, or five items in a list, then organized them according to some pattern, say, from smallest to largest, or vice versa. My impaired ability to collect and remember new information was a deficit which became increasingly apparent as my other injuries healed, and the anxiety it gave me was far different from my other fears. I always had a keen ability to retain facts and have them readily available at a moment's notice; it served me particularly well throughout college and graduate school, and it was a definite asset in the business world as well. In 1987 I found myself grasping for the simplest details of the day before. Names, which had never been a problem, now seemed to elude me. My short-term memory was in shambles too, and I was very much aware of this. I couldn't remember from therapy to therapy what I had done. Moreover, recalling what I had done in a particular therapy session, trying to dictate a few summary notes to my therapist to write in my log, an exercise we often used to end a session, was a halting struggle. This inability to recall what I had just done frightened me to the point of tears. "If only I could see," I thought, "I could take and read my own notes."

Yet I knew this was impossible — at the moment. I could hardly make out objects, let alone read my own ragged printing. I flatly refused when anyone suggested that I use a tape recorder. "I will see again! I will! I will!" I cried to my parents. I fought any suggestion that I might simply adapt to my eyesight and get on with my life. "There has to be some way of regaining what I lost. I'm not strong enough to go through life like this," I told my parents. I was desperate at the thought of never seeing clearly again, and I was increasingly aware that the "It's broke, and we can't fix it," attitude prevailed among most medical and rehabilitation environments.

I kept practicing with my sweatshirt. My therapist wrote out the sequence and steps again and reviewed them with me. Having more or less mastered the right, I moved on to trying to identify objects with my left hand. This was so difficult that I felt like a failure again. I practiced more memory strategies, forcing myself to paint a picture in my head, meticulously trying to store information. I tried reading short words, all printed in different-sized types. I could read three-letter words that were at least 1/4 inch tall, but I had difficulty with four- and five-letter words. I had to relearn how to "see" a word, how to start at the left hand side and move right. My therapist used a blue line at the beginning of each word, helping me remember to start at the left. I worked at regaining control over my left arm, and I practiced using it to grasp and release objects. In one exercise, I worked on opening the toothpaste and putting some on a toothbrush, over and over.

In other exercises, a therapist read something out loud to me, and I worked at understanding and remembering as much information as possible. One day we worked through two paragraphs, my therapist reading slowly, me listening and trying to paint a visual image of each detail she mentioned. This time I recalled almost all the information, both immediately following the reading and after a short break. Finally, now that I could be reasonably sure of recalling information I had just learned, I was ready to move on to formal problem-solving exercises. Again I learned the process: (1) Make sure you understand exactly what the problem asks; (2) Check all your options and weigh the pros and cons of each; (3) Choose the solution that seems best; and (4) Check yourself for accuracy. I was beginning to feel I could really think again, if only at a very basic level.

Valentine's day weekend I spent at home. At this time, using my therapist's instructions, I could readily put my pants on, but my blouse almost defeated me. I kept missing the left sleeve. In my journal, my father noted: "Using her crutch, Joan walked out the front door, one step onto the stoop, one step down to the walk, then walked 25 feet and down the four steps to driveway. She walked around on driveway and to rear of house, about 400 feet total. Joan was well-pleased, and the fresh air was excellent."

This weekend was especially significant, because it was the first time I actually wanted to venture outside. The fresh air was invigorating, and I still remember how wonderful the wind felt as it blew against my face. I remember, too, consciously limiting time outside because I didn't want the neighbors to see me. I imagined how pathetic I looked, and I was afraid that someone might venture outside to talk with me, and conversation was the last thing I wanted.

The selfishness and pride that permitted me to isolate myself are still vivid. Daily I struggled to maintain what little dignity seemed left to me. I was ferociously protective of my privacy. I told my parents repeatedly that, "I'm not going to inflict myself on anyone." I felt comfortable only around my parents and my therapists. They understood how and what I was, and they accepted me as I was. In the following months, I let others in only slowly, as I learned to trust again. Developing an ability to trust others enough to be vulnerable with them was a long and difficult struggle, and one I'd never undergone before. Before my accident, I responded to other people from my own sense of strength. After the accident, when I was so aware of my dependence and neediness, I didn't trust others to readily accept me. I didn't want their pity, and I didn't want anyone to feel that they had to accept me as I was; it seemed far too much to ask. At the same time, I think it is much harder for the people around us to watch someone they love suffer than it is to actually go through pain oneself. The onlookers feel a similar helplessness and a similar anger. No one prepares a family or a friend for such a traumatizing experience. My friend Michael, whom I cared for so much, suffered this same pain. I have no recollection of his early visits, and I think he needed me to know he was present, needed me to acknowledge his own pain. Once at Harmarville, I denied my situation and my needs for many weeks. During the first visit with him I can remember, I told him that I had no idea why I was "in this place," and I was determined to get out — fast. I think Michael didn't know the person who spoke to him, and he didn't know how to respond to her.

All in all, I saw him very little during the first two years of my recovery, and that distance was my choice. It was easier for both of us, I rationalized, if he didn't see my struggle. I didn't want him to see me struggling to relearn things I had accomplished 18 years ago, and I didn't want to go through the mental exhaustion and discomfort that characterized our few visits together. Talking to him was much easier by phone; I could mask my true emotions — so often despair and thoughts of just "ending this nightmare by ending it all" — in a cheery voice over the phone. I felt he wasn't fooled in the least, but I denied this knowledge as well. I was so consumed by my blindness that I couldn't think about Michael and the pain I knew he was experiencing as well. I think it was my inability to accept my own vulnerability, along with his feeling that I seemed unable to rise to this, my toughest challenge, that finally unravelled our relationship. I made a conscious choice to limit his participation in my healing and rehabilitation, and he did not protest.

Pride, whoever it is directed at, is an awful thing. I was so ashamed of myself, and so enveloped in my own emotional pain, that I could not reach out to others or let them reach out to me. I avoided them before they could reject me, convincing myself they that would, because I'd rather be rejected than vulnerable. I was angry at them, angry at the potential dependency they seemed to represent.

Most of all, I was angry with God for allowing this horrible accident to happen to me. I could only yell at Him, repeatedly asking "Why?" I had always firmly believed in the maxim, "God helps those who help themselves." In those few most desperate moments when I did make an effort to approach God, I scorned my own efforts, chastising myself for thinking that God would help me, for hoping God might heal me. My faith was too weak, and it remained so for many months to come. I could not remain calm and complacent about my eyesight. I did not know how to ask God, simply and quietly, to help me. My requests were always tinged with rage. I was still horrified to find myself in this inescapably dependent predicament. I felt God knew my heart anyway, and he would see through my tears to the deep anger seething within me. "You could have prevented this," I said inside, "but You didn't."

That same weekend, I rose above my pride long enough to ambulate around the South Hills Mall with my crutch, rather than in a wheelchair, and I bought a pair of tennis shoes with velcro fasteners. The therapist who helped me dress had mentioned the new style, and, after considering what it would cost my ego, I asked my mother to take me out to look for them. At Kinney's we found a pair of white shoes with grey and pink racing stripes on each side. Fastening my own shoes gave me an increased sense of control, something I sorely craved, and my successful trip gave me an even greater sense of satisfaction. I needed to concentrate on the little things that gave me more independence; I concentrated on these "small" accomplishments and built on them.

Unfortunately, I continued to measure my accomplishments against the same standard I used before the accident, and, of course, I always fell short. This constant and destructive "measuring up" ceased only when I accepted a new set of standards, ones which had little to do with physical accomplishments, but everything to do with spiritual accomplishments. Indeed, I had a long road to travel.

By the end of February Dr. Reimer agreed that my right leg was strong enough to bear my full weight. I was officially exercising without my crutch for short periods. I spent five or ten minutes at a time on a nordic skier in the gym. I practiced several activities designed to test and improve my balance, including walking a straight line forward and backward, and "braiding," or placing one foot over the other while walking. I worked with a "balance beam," really nothing more than a two by four board, about ten feet long. On it I stood about three inches above the floor. I was to walk across the beam in a straight line, frontwards, backwards, and sideways, without falling off. I found these tasks extremely difficult, and my therapist attributed it to two reasons: Because of my poor vision and spatial deficits, I could not focus on the board in front of me; and due to the stroke, my left arm was hardly more than a dead weight, constantly pulling me off balance and causing me to fall to the left side. Often I was so angry and frustrated that I cried while I tried to walk along the beam. Even though I was aware of my progress (afterall, I was walking, and no longer strapped in a wheelchair), it seemed so small, and so useless. I wanted to quit, but I knew I couldn't. I can't claim the strength which saw me through these difficult months, a time where I encountered more failures than victories, and even the victories seemed meager.

February 25th was my birthday. I was 30 years old, a milestone for most people, I supposed. To me it seemed like one more marker of all I'd lost. I felt melancholy all day, reflecting on all the wonderful celebrations of my past birthdays — celebrations where I felt happy and loved. I didn't want a celebration this year; I certainly did not feel that I deserved to be loved. I didn't love this dependent, disoriented, disabled person who had lost control of her life, and if I didn't, how could I expect others to do so? I thought of the suffering my loved ones had undergone since my accident, and I added that to my guilt. Fear and self-pity gripped me. I told God, again, that it would have been better to let me die. I was angry, I was scared, and again I blamed God. I saw no promise for my future, and I felt no joy or thanks in my heart; only pain, surrounding the memories of who I had been. Again, God would be patient with my impatience and ignorance.

The next day, I threw myself back into my therapy. I tried to run errands — buying stamps, making change at the change machine, then purchasing a soda. Accomplishing this trivial list, with all the little steps that made up each task, was difficult. I forgot where the change machine was; I went back without the soda.

I also swam 30 laps, doing the crawl, losing myself in the motion of the water and my own body, working on lifting my weak left arm higher above the surface of the water and pulling harder with it. I swam on a weekly basis with several other patients. The exercise was excellent therapy for my arm, but even more beneficial to me mentally and emotionally. My body felt far less awkward and helpless in the water, and I could take pride in my progress as a swimmer. Each lap was a concrete, tangible achievement, and the water splashing around my face and ears gave me an illusion of privacy that was very rare. I sometimes think I got more out of swim therapy than I did out of all my exercises combined.

One entry in my journal read: February 27, 1987: "When dressing this morning, Joan had difficulty with pants because she did not want to put velcro on pants. Joan thought she could use tag on the pants to help her identify the back correctly, but she found that this was not as easy as she thought." As my father read this particular passage to me, I smiled. There was my headstrong, stubborn self in full display. I was determined to get dressed like a normal person, i.e., without any velcro tags for identification. My therapist allowed me to attempt putting on my pants without using the patch, as I usually did, to orient the front and the back. I failed at this first attempt, surprising no one but myself. But no matter; this was not my first failure at something I tried to do in my own way, and it certainly was not the last. I was angry, but not defeated. I needed a few more weeks of practice. I tried again and again over the weeks, struggling to put on my pants without using the velcro tag.

That same day, I practiced running errands again, remembering both the change and the soda, but forgetting the landmarks I used to find the change and soda machines. In the gym, I practiced throwing and catching a basketball with both hands.

For Monday, March 2, 1987, my journal read: "Joan had some difficulty identifying velcro on front of pants. Once identified, she put them on independently. She was able to lay out her top correctly on lap, but then had difficulty guiding left hand through sleeve." 9:00, Occupational Therapy: "Joan went on an errand to get stamps" (Stamps were sold within Harmarville, at a small office near the O.T. clinic). "She remembered the general area where the stamps are sold. Back in the clinic, she knew where the stamps should be placed, but she had difficulty getting them straight on the envelope." All a routine day's struggle, and yet, the second of each month marked another milestone for me as I counted the months since December 2, 1986, the day of the accident. This date meant three months had passed since the accident. Somehow it seemed much longer to me, as I settled further into the daily routine of my rehabilitation program.

That same week, I managed to put on my pants and socks and shoes by myself. The sweatshirt proved difficult again; lining it up correctly in relation to my body seemed a mysterious and frustrating riddle. My list of errands expanded to include trips to the cashier and the xerox machine. I began eating without assistance in my meal-group, and I planned to start eating in the cafeteria on Friday.

I also started a new class called "Home Management," which focused on skills such as cooking, washing, menu planning, and other tasks related to independence within the home. My first task was making a soft-boiled egg and tea. I had problems adjusting the timer for three minutes, and consequently, my egg was hard-boiled.

In the gym, I worked on the balance beam, which I was beginning to master. We played "catch" with a basketball while I stood on the beam. By this time I could stand and move fairly easily, but pivoting to catch the ball brought me down. In my journal, the Physical Therapist wrote "Joan promised to persevere." The comment seems characteristic of this new person I was becoming, but still curious. I can't remember if I was so angry the therapist had to extract this promise from me, or if I meant to show her my determination. In many ways, the woman described in this journal is still a stranger to me.

Whoever she was, she kept working, fueled by anger and doggedness, and a strange strength from a source she could not pinpoint. For Thursday, March 5, 1987 my log read: 7:00 — "Joan had some difficulty with her bra this morning. Pants were no problem. She was better able to visualize how her shirt should go on, which helped her to know when she was putting it on backwards." 9:00, Occupational Therapy — "Did some errands around the Center. Joan remembered both the errands she was to do. In the O.T. clinic, we worked on grasping, releasing, and controlling left arm movements." 10:00, Neuropsychology — "Worked on recognizing shapes, identifying their color, number, and location. Performance has significantly improved since similar test was conducted on January 19, 1987." 11:00, Home Management — "Practiced orientation to the kitchen. Joan made cup of tea with the hotshot beverage maker."

This last note might appear to underline a trivial accomplishment, but it was, in fact, a major accomplishment for me. I was beginning to slowly demonstrate my skill at some small tasks, such as making a cup of tea. I wasn't totally independent — I still required a therapist's supervision — but I was beginning to understand that with practice I could learn to do things for myself, and I was beginning to take some pride in that. I remained, however, my own worst critic, belittling myself for not making the tea more quickly and without cues from my therapist. Any excitement was always tempered by the insignificance of the task.

That evening, I received a phone call from Boulder, Colorado. The call was a surprise, and it was therapeutically valuable because it required me to recall information about my past work, and made me feel I might some day do it again.

As I noted earlier, IBM was in the process of moving to Boulder from Poughkeepsie at the time of my accident. I am told, although I don't recall, that I had made at least four business trips out to Boulder to interview and hire employees to staff the necessary positions of the Offshore Sales department, which I had managed in Poughkeepsie. I had decided not to relocate myself, believing that my next step should be to one of the World Trade headquarter locations in Tarrytown, New York. I still had the responsibility, however, of staffing the Offshore Sales department that would operate in Boulder.

Late that afternoon, the young woman who had been selected to manage the department staff called. I recognized her name at once, but I had difficulty visualizing her face. I remembered a young, blonde-haired woman named Kathy, self-confident, anxious to learn and ensure that the department I had once managed maintained the same level of service and standards it had attained in New York. Kathy began by leading me gently, making certain that I knew who she was, and the department she now headed. I thought, "What were these people told about my injuries?" I couldn't help but wonder if everyone was warned to handle Joan with kid gloves.

I quickly put those thoughts aside as Kathy began ticking off the names of people from the Boulder site that I had hired to staff positions. The names and the faces came clearly to mind as I began associating them with the specific job responsibilities for which I had hired them. This recollection and the revelation that I could still rely on my memory, however rusty, was a gift unlike any I had received in the past four months. I remember thanking Kathy over and over again, and telling her that she had no idea of how much she had helped me by calling. She triggered so much in my mind. After hanging up the phone, I sat in my wheelchair on one side of the open hallway. I let the tears fall freely. Everything seemed to come rushing back: memories of how I was as a manager, how much I had loved my work, and how much I missed it.

That weekend, my father and I visited Carnegie Library, in Oakland, searching for information on cortical blindness, which was the term I had come to associate with my particular visual deficit. My mind was filled with questions, all revolving around ways I could help "fix" my eyesight.

I wanted to learn all I could about cortical blindness and visual disorders following anoxic brain injury, and I wanted to uncover some information or technique that would lead to the restoration of my eyesight. But that day our library search proved fruitless; we found many books on the brain, but no detailed information on cortical blindness.

On Monday (my father often read to me) we began reading an article, "Disturbances of Visual Perception following Cerebral Lesions," written by Dr. Ratcliff, head of the neuropsychology department at Harmarville. We read that there are three types of perceptual deficits following damage to the posterior part of the brain; the one that seemed most like my perceptual problems was the second type, in which the basic deficit seems to be an impairment of the ability to process information about spatial relationships. I wanted to know all I could about my injury. Only then could I begin resolving my deficits — particularly my visual deficit. I thought understanding my injury would lead to resolving it.

I still used velcro tags on my pants and sweatshirt to correctly place them on my lap, but slowly and erratically I was improving. I struggled to remember from day to day the way to orient the clothing to my body. I still worked at donning my sweatshirt in Occupational Therapy, and I think my uneven progress was the result of sheer practice. As I learned my way around the grounds, I could usually remember my list of errands and my destinations, but I still had trouble locating the change machine. I played Rummy with my therapist, working to remember the rules.

My long-term memory appeared to be recovering steadily, but developing my short-term memory, which was key to recalling the steps just learned in a simple task — such as learning to play a game like Rummy 500 — remained a frustrating battle. I quivered at my inability to quickly recall the steps to a given task or the events of the day. I felt my sharp intellect was gone. I bristled with anger when therapists or doctors attempted to reassure me that memory deficits due to head injuries were "normal." "Well, they're not 'normal' for me!" I said to myself. "These people don't know me. They don't know what I am capable of doing. I'll show them! I'll show them all!" I still had a desperate need to feel I had some control over my life, and it was some time before I realized that I never really had the control I'd always imagined, and that I probably never would.

On March 16th, 1987, my father and I met with the doctor who headed the head-injury unit at Harmarville, to review my progress and give me a chance to question the doctor directly on my injuries. In my journal, my father summarized the meeting this way:

(1) Left arm will improve with therapy, but it will always be weak. Must establish brain-to-arm control for the fingers of the left hand.
(2) Eyesight should improve to the extent that Joan may read before she leaves Harmarville.
(3) Writing will improve as eyesight improves.
(4) Fine line writing will be read with the assistance of a ruler or other visual aid.
(5) Weaknesses: Concentrate on dressing, which remains a problem. Mind's eye orientation of clothing in relation to body is still difficult. Performing math problems in mind's eye also difficult.

For me, of course, my eyesight was the primary concern. I was confident I could resolve the balance and walking deficits, as well as strengthen my weak left arm, but my impaired vision frightened me; more than anything else, it seemed to threaten me with life-long dependency. I ignored the doctor's mention of visual aids and line guides to assist me with reading. I would settle for nothing less than the restoration of the eyesight I had lost.

This meeting resulted in a major advancement for me and my treatment plans. My deficits were pointed out in concrete, direct terms that I couldn't deny. Still I sought to fully recover from my deficits, and the doctor's summary gave me a solid checklist to measure myself against. I still refused any recommendations of adaptive equipment and strategies.

I believed the burden of achieving this goal fell directly on my shoulders, and that, despite all the people who surrounded me with help and support, I could trust only my own efforts to deliver myself from this situation. I didn't ask God again for the healing I so desperately wanted. I knew my earlier requests to Him had amounted to little more than demands. He didn't reply to my desperation, as far as I was concerned, and I decided that I wouldn't beg Him to restore what was taken from me any longer. I didn't blame God for His response (which I interpreted as ignoring me) because I knew all too well the many years in which I had ignored Him. Somehow, perhaps, I deserved this punishment. It was up to me to work at recovering myself, at recovering my vision. I had not yet learned to place my trust in a God who does not fail; I did not know Him, then. I set out to find the answers I desired on my own, just as I had always done.

The next day, Tuesday, I went back to my work. I kept trying to develop my functional memory skills, and I learned new strategies by reviewing basic information about the brain in general and the occipital lobes in particular. It was still difficult for me to recall the four lobes of the brain and locate them on a diagram, so I suggested we color-code the diagram, an old trick from my college studies. Since my therapy specified these memory exercises, I had asked my therapist if we could focus on information important to me, and important to my quest for a cure.

Later in the month, I went through tests again, trying to note my progress. One test tried to ascertain my strength in both arms. It was very hard to record my grip strength in my left hand, because it was still numb. I couldn't sense how hard I squeezed the hand meter. I also tried to read an eye chart, but I still couldn't identify even the largest letters at the top of the chart. I practiced tracing and drawing free hand basic geometric shapes. The latter was still difficult, but one old strategy, tracing the figure I wanted to draw with my finger first, seemed to increase my drawing accuracy.

On Tuesday, March 24, 1987, for the second time, I put my shirt and pants on with cues from the therapist, but without velcro tags. Four months after my injury, I finally felt that I had proved myself capable of dressing independently. No longer did I have to wait for someone to come dress me. Despite all my practice and determination, my success, coming after so many months of frustration, was probably due to how much I resented having to wait for a therapist to come and "cue" me on correct dressing. Patience was never my virtue, but I was slowly and angrily learning it. Even in this success, I was a little disheartened; I couldn't do such simple things without thinking, and I worried that they would never be simple again.

On April 15, 1987, I was formally dismissed as an inpatient from Harmarville. I had mixed emotions about my dismissal; I was happy to go home, eager for the freedom of a non-institutionalized environment, but I was worried and fearful, because I was leaving without having recovered my eyesight, and I could not give up hope of seeing clearly again. At the same time, I was excited over an appointment with a doctor whose name had been given to me by the staff at Harmarville. This doctor was a low-vision specialist, an optometrist with an excellent reputation for helping people with visual deficits — people like me, I was told.

I met this man two days later, on Good Friday, of all days. He was positive that he could help me. He placed a pair of telescopic lenses, attached to a clinical eyeglass frame on my eyes. The frame and the lenses were heavy against my cheekbones, and bulky. As I started to focus through the lenses, I began moving my head to scan the room, and I suddenly caught a glimpse of my father and my sister, who sat across from me. I remember gasping, for I saw them more clearly than I had in five months. I started to cry, and they did, too. The lenses didn't completely resolve the blurriness that obscured everything I saw. They were powerful, awkward, and they tended to give me a headache, but I was ecstatic, aware that with them I saw farther and sharper than I had in a long time.

Again, here was hope. A week later, I began a program with this doctor. His training concentrated initially on my ability to recognize letters and small words, then moved on to various adaptive equipment to assist me in seeing and reading more proficiently. Although, as always, I sought recovery of my eyesight, not adaptation, in my mind this was a start towards regaining the eyesight I had lost. I convinced myself that I would learn to use the adaptive equipment, but only in the interim, only until my full visual capacities were restored.

A GREATER VISION

CHAPTER FIVE

LIFE AS AN OUT-PATIENT

AS I SAID, MY FEELINGS ABOUT LEAVING Harmarville were very mixed. Although I had arranged to continue as an out-patient, the staff and my family urged me to "take a vacation," to give myself and my therapies a rest for a while. I felt as if I were working against a deadline, and as if every moment I spent not working toward recovery was wasted. At this point, taking a holiday seemed extravagant.

In many ways, being home felt wonderful. Jeanie was home, and her brilliant, acid humor was like a tonic to me. We all attended Easter Mass, then we went to visit my grandparents, where we had dinner together. All these traditions reminded me of our past holidays, and although I never forgot that my life wasn't the same, this Easter was another homecoming for me.

Throughout my "vacation," I tried hard to take it easy, and to adjust to living at home. I took over my old upstairs bedroom and spent time re-arranging my things, organizing them so that I could find everything easily. I slept in my own bed, more or less set my own schedule, and ate my mother's cooking. It was a relief to be free of Harmarville's institutional schedule. Now that there was no staff to be cheerful for, I cried unaccountably and often, mourning my changed life. My parents, understanding that I needed this time and this sadness, didn't try to comfort me, or reveal how my unhappiness hurt them. In the following months, they supported every plan, every therapy I tried. Despite the negative predictions my doctors made, they never suggested that I wouldn't completely regain my sight; they took my goal and made it theirs completely, as no one else did.

Still, I chafed at my position in the house. I was like a child again, unable to do the simplest things without my mother's help. To me it seemed that she took up our old mother-daughter roles eagerly, with relief. She was always available, combing and curling my hair, reaching things I couldn't, making me snacks and cleaning up after me, on and on. The list of things I was unable to do seemed endless, and, bitterly aware of how much I needed her help, I couldn't help resenting her part in each one.

I remembered the day my parents dropped me off at Penn State when I enrolled as an undergraduate. I was the first person in our family to go to college, and I was moving away from home for the first time. I felt unique and ecstatic, eager to begin this new stage in my life alone. As they left, my mother forced a cautious smile, trying hard to acknowledge my excitement, but she knew our relationship was changed forever, and I think she regretted it. But here I was, ten years later, home again, her "child" again, in a way I'd never imagined. I both hated and valued the intimacy that developed between us during this time.

My parents attended Mass every Sunday and, because I lived in their house, I attended with them. I disliked going, in part because it seemed one more sign of my childish life in their house. Sitting in Robinson Township's Holy Trinity Catholic Church each week, I felt cold inside, and bitterly separated from the people around me as well as God. All my prayers were the same grudging, angry requests: "Let me see again." I felt no comfort, no uplift, only impatience — I was wasting time better spent practicing the letters of the alphabet and simple math.

Although I didn't realize it at the time, Sister Agnes, the woman in our parish who prayed for me when I was in a coma at Allegheny General, watched me from a distance, noting my progress as I moved from my wheelchair and short visits home to walking and living at home. We still knew very little about each other, and, at this time, I made no move to lessen that distance.

Thursday, April 30, 1987 was the first day of my rehabilitation program as an out-patient at Harmarville. My father drove me there to continue my therapy five days a week. Becoming an outpatient made me feel I had more control over my life and over the therapy methods offered me. As far as I was concerned, achieving recovery was my responsibility. I spent every working moment at some type of exercise or therapeutic activity. I continued developing my problem-solving capacity, focusing on word problems and deductive reasoning. I bought flash-cards to use for both visual and mathematical drill work. I asked my father to build a balance beam for me, a long plank of wood on which I could practice. I even practiced folding towels at home, striving to match the corners evenly, until I was exhausted. Although I was painfully aware of all my deficits, I continued to care most about my eyesight, and getting it back was the most important goal in my life. I was prepared to work until I was fully capable, no longer legally blind and back at IBM. Before long, my neuropsychology therapist, who sensed that I was in overdrive (more a case of overkill), warned me to slow down before I burned out.

Aware that there was truth in her warnings, I agreed to consciously set aside some time for listening to music or calling a friend, for something relaxing, even if I couldn't let myself enjoy it. My mind was always fixed on what exercise I was neglecting or overlooking, what other activity might move me towards recovery.

I was determined to escape my situation on my own power and return to the life I had known. My pride prevented me from approaching the one who could have helped me most, and, in a way, my soul yearned to approach Him. God knew how I loathed asking for anything I felt I should be able to accomplish on my own. Despite the strides I made in my physical and cognitive recovery, I had miles to go in my spiritual recovery. I had to rid myself of the self-pitying thought that God was on an active campaign to make my life miserable, and I had to recognize that He was not rejecting me, but I was rejecting what He wanted to give me.

I clung to my past, knowing well that I was not ready, at this time, to think of my future without all the things I had already attained. My career was, after all, where I had performed best; it was the arena that groomed and challenged my talents, and it was the environment I wanted to re-enter. I gave no thought to any other alternative; as far as I was concerned, there was none. It was many months before I understood that "when God closes a door, He opens a window." I was not ready to accept the closed doors I saw in my life. I wanted only to bust them wide open with the rage that was bottled up inside me.

For some time I continued a program with the low vision specialist I first met on Good Friday, and I went to his office each Monday morning at 9:00 to work with his wife on low-vision training. I initially trained with a patch covering my left eye, attempting to read letters ranging from 3 millimeters to 1.5 millimeters in size. Within two weeks, I was reading four and five-letter words which were 3 millimeters tall, proving to myself, as well as others, that I could read — even if the words were small in length and somewhat large in size. Seeing that I could do this much, even though I couldn't read as easily or accurately as I wanted, allowed me to believe that the doctors who told me that I would never see clearly again — at least not without the use of a visual aid for reading — were mistaken. I was struggling to read, but I was reading. "I'll prove them wrong," I still told myself over and over again.

I chose not to hope for a miracle from God; while I believed miracles certainly could occur, I had no hopes of experiencing such Divine intervention. Knowing well my years of ignorance and my neglect of God, I did not dare approach Him for what I wanted. I was not quite convinced that, in 1987, God still performed miracles. I knew about Christ's healing in the Bible, and I believed in the miracles and healing He performed while He walked this earth. But I doubted that miracles occurred in 1987. "Healing only occurred to really holy people, anyway," I thought. I certainly wasn't holy, or even close to holiness. God knew me only too well.

Although I never thought God caused my accident, I knew that He had permitted it to happen, that He could have prevented it, but didn't, and I couldn't understand why. I couldn't really pray — I couldn't share in the mutual communication possible with God. I was too hurt, and too angry. At that time, any conversation I initiated with God was a one-sided shouting match, usually manifested when I was again stymied by some small thing I had once done without hesitation. I continued to hold before me memories of my former life, as well as the knowledge that I had been stripped of it.

Soon after the accident, my sister Jeanie had urged my family to engage a lawyer. He attempted to prosecute the man who caused my accident, but because of a lack of evidence — his initial hit-and-run tactics served him well — he could not be criminally prosecuted. Our lawyer also contacted and sued the company the man drove for, and he learned that during the initial investigation the driver quit. Rage, laced with bitterness, set in again when I learned from my lawyer that the driver responsible for causing my accident was now driving for another company. I was furious with him, and with a society that so carelessly acknowledged what he had done to my life.

But now we found he was driving again. "He's still out on the road," I cried to my parents. "There's no justice in any of this nightmare." I was left to deal with the handicaps imposed upon me by that driver's carelessness, and he was permitted back on the road, as if his life had never damaged mine? "I hate that man who did this to me!" I cried repeatedly. I couldn't believe the injustice of it all. I didn't understand that there truly is very little justice in this world, or that I must look elsewhere for a greater, more complex justice.

My left hand and arm improved only slowly. I could usually discern sharp stimuli, like a pin prick or the feel of a metal object, but I usually could not distinguish hot from cold. When I asked, my therapist told me I'd never have sensory ability in my left hand that I once had, but that it might still improve.

For Thursday, May 21, 1987 my neuropsychology therapist wrote in my log: "Joan worked on tough problem-solving exercise. It took her almost 45 minutes to solve a similar problem three weeks ago, and under three minutes today. Nice, steady improvement. Don't give up."

Many times I wanted to give up. My progress was painfully slow, and I was nowhere near where I wanted to be. I was walking better, my problem-solving and cognitive abilities were improving, and I was progressing in my low-vision training. Yet six months after my accident, I was very much aware that my progress was far slower than I'd hoped. I was especially concerned that my vision had improved very little, and I clung to the words of those therapists and doctors who stressed that I was still "early in recovery." I interpreted those words to mean that there was still time, that I shouldn't expect a "full" recovery of what I had lost *yet*.

I looked at every accomplishment as my own, borne or failed of my own endeavors. In doing so, I didn't credit the One responsible for permitting all my achievements. Again, God waited patiently for Joan to acknowledge Him in the way He so rightly deserved.

On June 25, 1987, Dr. Diamond, the physician who headed my case at Allegheny General, called to inform us that I was no longer required to take Cumiden, the anti-coagulant medication prescribed for me since my transfer from Allegheny General Hospital to Harmarville. Since the accident, I'd had blood tests every week, for Dr. Diamond closely monitored my blood chemistry and the possibility of more clotting occurring in the arteries of my neck. In the early weeks after the accident, doctors advised my parents that I would need Cumiden medication for the rest of my life. Another medical prognosis unfulfilled. I've remained medication-free since that date.

I continued my out-patient therapy at Harmarville through the summer, making small but consistent progress in my walking, my balance, and in my cognitive abilities. I also continued my work in the low-vision program. Sometime during that summer, I overheard discussions among nurses and therapists about patients who had "plateaued," who had stopped improving through therapy, and they often noted that training with adaptive devices was the patient's "only hope" of simulating a "normal" life. I grew concerned with the routine into which I'd "settled," and I was terrified of hearing that dreadful word, "plateau," applied to me. To me, adaptive equipment still signified throwing in the towel, succumbing to the crews of doctors, nurses and therapists and agreeing that somehow they'd all been right, that I would never see clearly again and never regain the full use of my left hand.

I didn't buy it. The doctors had been wrong about me, before, and I believed I could prove them wrong again. Even my low-vision doctor, skilled in the use of adaptive devices, talked to me about the "structuralists" in the medical profession, those doctors who adopted an adaptive rather than curative attitude to brain-injury. "How can they be so matter-of-fact with people's lives?" I asked myself. "Who made them God?"

In the fall of 1987, I contacted the neuropsychologist who worked at retraining the visual capacity lost during anoxic brain injury. Her work had been documented in an article given to me months earlier — the same article my own neuro-opthamologist had dismissed with a brusque "they do quirky things." This neuropsychologist had worked with a young girl diagnosed as cortically blind, a term I adopted in describing my own impairment. The article described the treatment which reportedly resulted in restoration of the girl's visual capacities and her return to school, where she could read and write without visual aids. I contacted this neuropsychologist directly, explaining, as best I could, my visual deficits and other disabilities.

I was desperate, looking for any hope of recovering my vision. She offered to visit Pittsburgh and conduct an evaluation on me in my parents' home, which spanned over three days. During that time, she performed a series of neuropsychological evaluations. Before she left, we agreed on a program of therapies designed by her and administered by my father at home. He recorded my performance on certain tasks which she designed for me, then mailed the results to her. Although it was clear we would have a long-distance relationship at best, I was anxious to begin what she termed a "remediation program." Remediation refers to the process of educating, of remedying or overcoming disabilities. Generally the idea was to "retrain" the remaining tissue in the occipital areas of my brain, overcoming my injuries by simply bypassing the damaged tissue, substituting another neural pathway for the old one. Many of the exercises were similar to ones I already did at Harmarville: I traced figures and letters, alternating between relearning the shape itself and attempting to reproduce it. She made no definite promises, but she said she was hopeful about my ability to recover the capacities lost as a result of my injury.

In a letter to my lawyer, a response to his request for information on the results of her evaluation, she wrote the following:

> This letter is a follow-up to our phone conversation, and your letter, in which you requested information about the results of my evaluation, the future probable course of Joan's condition, and any other data that might be helpful.
>
> Joan Ulicny is a thirty year old white female, who was involved in a motor vehicle accident on December 2, 1986. As a result of that injury, she sustained a closed-head injury, bilateral occipital lobe infarcts, and right hemispheric parietal damage. Reported neuropsychological deficits include hemiparesis of the left arm, neglect, memory disturbance, and cortical blindness.

84

When I arrived in Pittsburgh, I was met by both Joan and her father at the local airport. It was apparent that Joan had residual, functional vision; she was able to walk through the airport, negotiate stairways, and get into an automobile. She appeared to have difficulties 'focusing' when speaking to me. I evaluated Joan from September 23 to September 26. Neuropsychological evaluation consisted of administering measures of intelligence, memory, perception, sensation, and motor abilities.

Joan was attentive and cooperative throughout the testing. She showed no difficulty in comprehending task instructions or responding verbally to tasks. She was highly motivated throughout the testing.

Evaluation of intelligence with the Wechsler Adult Intelligence Scale showed a verbal I.Q. of 113 (bright/normal range of abilities), a performance I.Q. of 58 (in the mentally retarded range of abilities) and a full-scale I.Q. of 85 (low/average range of abilities) ....Visual-perceptual and visuo-motor deficits resulting from localized occipital and parietal disfunction may explain the low results on performance measures. Assessment with the Mini-Mental State Exam showed that Joan was oriented to time and place, could register auditory-verbal information, and that she had no gross attentional or language deficits. She could copy a short sentence; however, she was unable to draw a simple figure.

Standardized tests of reading showed performance on the WRAT at a third grade level. Spelling, as assessed by the WRAT was at a twelfth grade level....Tactile astereognosis was obtained in the left hand. The patient could not name objects presented after feeling them. She could name objects presented to the right hand. She could not identify which fingers of the left hand were being passively moved by the examiner. She could not accurately perform sequential and reversible oppositional movements involving the digits of the left hand ... In short, neuropsychological evaluation shows a thirty year-old female with resolving cortical blindness and left hemiparesis, no auditory verbal-language deficits, above normal verbal intelligence and a pattern of intellectual, memory perceptual deficits characteristic of bilateral occipital, right parietal and right frontal disfunction. It is predicted that a remediation program addressing specific components of visual, visuo-motor, tactile and motor deficits will result in changes in those domains.

Her report seemed accurate, and, in her description of my injuries, she confirmed many observations made by my other doctors. Her report differed because she suggested hope, however slight, that my vision would improve. As I said before, she made no definite promises that my eyesight or the sensation in my left hand would be restored. I chose to concentrate on the hope that a program developed by her might provide the method to recovery I searched for. I was anxious to start working on the program, and I turned deaf ears towards anything or anyone who reminded me that there was no strong evidence confirming such therapy. I saw hope, and I meant to pursue that hope in my own way, for as long as it took to recover my eyesight. I added these new exercises, adding another two hours to my training schedule every day. Once again, I was ready to accept the slightest suggestion of hope from anyone but God.

Even five months after I had made a conscious decision not to bother Him anymore, I still presented God with my needy anger. I felt I must sound like a broken record to Him. In fact, I kept this picture in my mind: There was God, in heaven, hearing my cries and anger and saying, "Oh, it's Joan in Pittsburgh, again." Sounding exhausted, He would add, "I wonder what she wants now?" I did not have the grace to understand God's mercy and endless love, or to realize that He was responding to me. Immersed in my own pain, I was not convinced that I could trust God for the help I needed, even though He had given me back my life when science and medicine had given my family little hope.

I continued my therapy at Harmarville while working both with the low-vision specialist and with the neuropsychologist on the at-home program. My abilities improved, but I was never satisfied with my progress. In my mind, I should have been leaps and bounds beyond the small gains I made. Everyone encouraged me to embrace these improvements and to be grateful for them, but I measured my thankfulness in terms of what my talents had allowed me to achieve — both at school and in my career. In these environments, I always looked to raise the bar higher, to challenge myself a little more, in order to accomplish more. That strategy had always worked for me before, but I slowly became aware that it might not work this time. Somewhere inside, although I never voiced the feeling, I knew that all the hard work and drive that characterized my character might fail me. Although the neuropsychologist assured me that I was making progress, I could discern no real difference in my abilities after working with her for several months. In my work with the low vision specialist, I reluctantly began to make use of some reading aids — only temporarily, I told myself, only until my vision returned. Because I couldn't focus on and follow a straight line, I couldn't easily follow a printed line of text or write in a straight line — I ended up with letters all over the page. To combat this, I used a "line guide" which highlighted one sentence at a time, but I had to stop and shift it for every line, an awkward and exasperating process. Eventually, Dr. Freeman also collaborated with IBM, producing a computer program that displayed each word of a text in three inch letters. With this program, I was able to write a little more quickly and independently, and in the coming year, God made this too a part of His plan.

There is a line in a prayer, "The Magnificat" (St. Luke 1:46-54), that states, "He will scatter the proud in the conceit of their hearts." God used the very things I based my self-understanding on, the very things I considered strengths, to show me my weaknesses. I didn't understand — in fact, I was incapable of understanding — the barrier I had put between myself and God. I had to recognize that my pride hindered my approaching, unconditionally, the One who could help me most. I did not know how to talk to God in humility and ask Him gently for His help. My attempts at asking God for assistance were too often couched in rage, and always centered only on what He could do for me, never what I might do for Him. Before the accident, I had seriously limited my prayer life, and I was not sure how to approach God for what I so desperately wanted. Prayers were something I said, something I expected to be heard, rather than something I truly listened to.

Finally, instead of questioning why He had not let me die, I began asking why He had permitted me to live. I found myself telling God that I did not know why He had spared my life, that I needed His help in learning to trust Him in what I knew would be difficult months ahead. God continually tested that new trust in the agonizing months that followed, but there was no other way to teach me. In doing so, He made me see, not only how much I needed Him, but how much I wanted Him in my life. Change came slowly as I moved towards His plan for me, but it came.

Externally, nothing else really changed. I continued with my out-patient therapy at Harmarville and the neuropsychologist's home program. I still applied my overkill strategy; I still believed the harder I worked myself, the sooner I'd outgrow my therapies, and the sooner I'd regain the capacities I had lost, especially my eyesight.

Only one other event hinted at my forthcoming spiritual recovery. One evening, my father read to me an article in the newspaper which became the seed of a monumental change in my life. I was led onto a path from which there was no return to the life I knew — one I could never have approached prior to my accident: a path of spiritual change, a path of conversion. I learned of a tiny, remote village in Yugoslavia called Medjugorje, and the events that had transpired there since 1981.

No matter what is taken away from you, if you keep your eyes on Jesus and praise Him, He will restore it to you. you will be joyful to the exact, same degree you have hurt. What you have lost, will be replaced ... joy for mourning ... beauty for ashes ... God, I don't see how it could possibly work now. I don't see how you will ever come to me again in any shape or form. But I won't limit you, so I'm going to remember this moment for the rest of my life. And if, and when, you restore the years that the locusts have eaten, I will tell people about it, and write about it. I am committing to you to remember this agony, and if you can come up with some kind of joy to the equivalent that I have hurt, you are truly a God of miracles.

— Writer Unknown

A GREATER VISION

PART TWO

WHEN I FIRST BEGAN THIS BOOK, I thought Chapter Two would be the most difficult to write, in part because I based my story mostly on other sources, medical and police accounts, and the stories of my family and friends, rather than on my own memory. Emotionally, it was the most difficult; in it I confronted the reality that I almost lost my life, and lost almost everything that seemed important to me. Intellectually, however, the period of my life covered in Part Two was hardest to describe. No explanation of a miracle can ever convince the intellect. That ever-prevailing human condition, skepticism, prevents us from accepting miracles, particularly in this century. In a world so ready to admire itself for numerous scientific and medical discoveries and other technological breakthroughs, the role of God in the universe has been treated as relatively insignificant.

If one first defines a miracle as a phenomenon that can't be explained in terms of the human condition, if one then defines it further, as I choose to do, as a beautiful grace from God, a rush of skeptics appear, all with prepared explanations, all backed by scientific studies, all anxious to disprove any idea of a miracle, and any connection God might have with it. The world is quick to discard the hand most able to help in all its ills; this knowledge amazes and pains me, but my own experience is the source of it. When I began writing this chapter, I felt tentative. Not because I doubted that the events in Medjugorje are of God, but because my intellect wanted to present as clearly, eloquently and definitely as possible, a credible explanation of what occurs in this small village; I wish all might accept this miracle as I have.

Yet I know my role is not to convince or persuade anyone to believe as I do. I don't believe that anything I write could change a person's life the way this knowledge has changed mine — only God does that. My purpose is to share one woman's experience and the role my re-awakened faith has played in my recovery in these recent years. I can't tell my story without emphasizing how my experience of the events in Medjugorje has brought God to the center of my life, a place which rightly belongs to Him. I didn't actively search for the faith that has manifested itself so strongly, and I haven't come along this path easily or willingly. In fact, in hindsight, I think I resisted this path years before my accident, and for more than a year after it. I had to learn to think with my heart, and not my intellect, not an easy feat for someone who based her sense of purpose and direction on her own will only. Yet I have come to desire only the clear intellect of a mind focused firmly on God. I still believe experience is always the most effective teacher, and I hope I can present my experiences as effectively as possible. To this end, I ask the reader to do what I couldn't for so many years: to think with her heart rather than her intellect. I found I had to learn to trust God again, and to trust in the greatest message of hope that God has sent the world since the birth of His only Son.

CHAPTER SIX

MEDJUGORJE:
AN ANSWER FROM ABOVE?

ONE BLUSTERY MORNING IN JANUARY of 1988, my father and I sat in the family room while he read me an article, "Medical Mystery?" which told of a woman from the Pittsburgh area who had been healed of multiple sclerosis. Her name was Rita Klaus. Apparently she suffered from MS for twenty years, but she claimed her affliction spontaneously disappeared in June of 1986, and she attributed her recovery to the reported apparitions of the Blessed Virgin Mary in Medjugorje, Yugoslavia. According to the article, she was one of the two or three Americans who traced their healings to the Medjugorje events, and doctors were befuddled by her inexplicable recovery. Six months after she had heard of Medjugorje and started following the directives of the Blessed Mother, Mrs. Klaus found herself free of her affliction, with no residual effects of MS apparent.

When we talked about the article, I told my father I believed miracles of physical healing could happen, but the article had also mentioned that Mrs. Klaus had studied, at one time, to be a nun. I thought her healing was probably due to the special graces God bestowed on her because she had once dedicated herself to this holy goal. In my mind, she had been healed because she had once made a conscious decision to give her life to Christ. Although the article stated that she received a dispensation from her vows when she was diagnosed with MS, left the convent and married, she must have been very special to

God for choosing this vocation, and He must have loved her very much. I was certainly no candidate for the same kind of grace. I put the article away, thinking "How wonderful for Mrs. Klaus," and didn't dwell on it any longer.

The truth was that I had pretty much fallen away from my faith in the last six or seven years before my accident. I disagreed with the Catholic Church on more than a few issues, and I had more or less become one of those "shopping cart" Catholics, picking and choosing from church doctrine for what I would adhere to and what I would reject. I tried to mold the Church and its teachings to my way of thinking. I was an "eighties" woman, after all: I felt myself — any woman — capable of any goal she might set for herself, and entitled to achieve any goal she might choose. I resented being expected to follow traditions that seemed ancient and inessential to my world.

I had always been a bit of a rebel, resenting any individual or organization which attempted to dictate my personal life. I rebelled against the Catholic Church by simply not attending, or by going only "when I had time," which meant very rarely. I hadn't been to confession for years, since before they started calling it the Sacrament of Reconciliation. "Why tell my sins to a man?" I thought. "My sins are between God and me." Quite some time passed before the bond between myself and my faith was restored, and, although I didn't recognize it at the time, Medjugorjie was the catalyst in resurrecting and recharging my faith.

Early in 1988, I made two trips back to Poughkeepsie. At that time, only another doctor and my concern for my eyes prompted me to go back there unhealed. It was as if my old life waited there for me, and I didn't want to return until I was ready to take up my career again. Sometimes I imagined my condominium holding all the things that had surrounded my life, the evidence of all I'd worked for. I still paid the bills, kept the power and the phone connected, kept my place vacant and waiting for me. Michael often went by to check on it for me, although we rarely talked to each other now. I still believed that I would heal myself, get my vision back, and return to my job in the near future. Perhaps even more than I hoped to return, I hated the thought of anyone else living in my space.

I made an appointment with the opthomologist I'd seen there, Dr. Praeger. That time — only a few months before the accident that changed my life — seemed so distant. Ironically, I had been in an earlier auto accident in 1985. Initially I thought I was uninjured, but several months later I found that any jarring motion, such as the exercises in my aerobics class, sent flashes of light across my left eye. In August of 1986, Dr. Praeger diagnosed a detached retina, and referred me to Dr. Hofeldt who repaired it. Dr. Prager also noted that my right eye might exhibit some damage in the future, and he suggested that I have it treated as well, just to be safe. But before I could make plans for my second surgery, God made other plans for my life.

My reading exercises and my work with the low-vision specialist seemed to be doing little good, and I decided to see Dr. Praeger for a check-up, to see if he thought this second laser surgery was still necessary, and, of course, on the slim chance that he might have something new to say about my blindness. My mother and I flew up for the appointment and flew back on the same day. I didn't want to stay in Poughkeepsie, even overnight. Every minute there was a confrontation with my own helplessness and with the obstacles that stood between me and my old life.

Dr. Prager examined me, again urging me to have the second laser treatment, and I agreed. It was good to talk with him again, but he could offer no new approach to healing my blindness. We scheduled the surgery for February 22nd. Mom and I made plans to return. For that trip, we would have to stay overnight in Poughkeepsie. The length of the surgery and the flight schedule made returning the same day impossible. Reluctantly, I decided we should stay at my condominium. After all, there were a few things I could pick up, and it *was* available.

A couple of weeks before this second visit, I heard of Medjugorje again. This time Sister Agnes, from our church, called to tell me that Rita Klaus, and a man named Wayne Weible, a former newspaper owner and publisher, would talk on Medjugorje at St. Mary's church in Beaver Falls on February 14, 1988. She asked if my father and I would like to go.

I thought, "Well, why not? I certainly don't have anything else planned for Valentine's Day." I was curious about Rita Klaus' story; I wanted to hear how she first learned of Medjugorje, and what it was, exactly, that she did to totally recover from MS.

The church was very crowded, and I wasn't close enough to see the two speakers at all. I could hear quite well, however, and I sat forward and listened attentively as Wayne Weible began to speak. He described his own conversion, and I could hear that his words were heart-felt.

As a Lutheran, he said, he didn't really know Mary; of course, he knew that She was the Mother of Christ, but otherwise his knowledge of Her was very limited. In his church She was mentioned at Christmas, but there was no elaboration of Her role in a worshiper's faith. Nevertheless, she asked him to make the spreading of Her messages at Medjugorje his life's work, and, as alien as this request and this career sounded to him, he had done so since 1986. First he wrote a series of columns about Medjugorje, then he printed a few thousand copies, planning to distribute them only in his home town area of South Carolina. At that time, he imagined his writing as nothing more than a Christmas story. By February 14, 1988, over ten million copies had been sent out all over the world. "How did this happen?" he asked. "It was never planned, and yet it happened."

I don't think there was one person in that audience who wasn't moved by his testimony, or one who doubted his sincerity or the truth of his words. Spreading Her messages of Medjugorje had, indeed, become Mr. Weible's life's work.

He was followed by Rita Klaus, a tall, statuesque woman who still lived in the Pittsburgh area. She began her talk with much of the material that had been included in the article, saying she'd suffered from MS for over twenty years, and describing the disease's progression to us. As her handicaps and her despondency increased, she became increasingly bitter, and she thought God no longer loved her. She was so angry with God and with herself that she could no longer pray.

At this statement, my attention rocketed. She, too, had felt abandoned by God, and she had felt that He no longer loved her. "She truly is a 'normal' person," I thought, "she thought God had quit on her, too."

Rita went on to tell how she'd first learned of Medjugorje, and how she began following the directives given by the Blessed Mother in Her messages to the visionaries in Medjugorje, six young people who saw and spoke with the Madonna daily. These messages were translated to the world weekly at first, then on a monthly basis. Rita stressed that she had never been to Medjugorje prior to her healing; she simply followed the guidance of the Blessed Mother, which centered on prayer, peace, fasting, penance, reconciliation with God and man, and conversion. This message seemed very simple, and I realized that it was really nothing new. I had been taught all these practices, as well as their importance, in religion classes during my twelve years of Catholic schooling, but I hadn't consciously applied those teachings in my own life for years. Listening to Rita, I thought, "they seemed so unnecessary."

Rita explained that she began fasting on Wednesdays and Fridays, saying the Rosary, and attending Mass daily. Six months later, she found herself totally free of her afflictions. Her story was beautiful and miraculous, and it confounded her doctors — they had no rationale for the fact that she was free from multiple sclerosis. As she described this change in her life, Rita seemed to shy away from the word "miracle." Instead, she described what happened to her as a "beautiful grace from God."

"There's that word again," I thought. "Grace, 'Amazing Grace,' as the song said. How can I get some of that grace?" Vaguely I remembered my early religion classes and that little blue Catechism book, which said that one way to attain grace was to receive the Sacraments. Although lately I had received Communion at Mass on Sundays, I realized that I hadn't received it with a pure heart. I hadn't been to confession in years — in my interpretation of Catholicism, it didn't seem necessary. Since my accident I had been too angry with God to examine my approach to Him. Before my accident, I just didn't care. However, as I listened to Rita I felt perhaps I needed to look at my relationship with God more closely, with something other than my anger. Shortly after attending the talks, I went to confession. For the first time, I was aware that I needed to be reconciled with God. If understanding my life and God's plan for it was possible, it would have to begin with a renewed relationship between us.

At the end of February, I returned to Poughkeepsie for my laser surgery appointment. I told none of my old friends, including Michael, that I would be in town. I didn't want to see anyone, and more importantly, I didn't want anyone to see me. I was still bitterly ashamed of my appearance, and these people knew the "old Joan," the one I consistently measured myself against. I was sure they would make the same comparisons, and I dreaded this trip.

The laser surgery went well and quickly, and afterwards my mother and I took a taxi to Fishkill, the little town outside of Poughkeepsie where I lived. I'd made this drive many times before, on my way home from work, and although it felt achingly familiar, my blurry vision and my sense of loss made it all seem distant at the same time.

As we pulled into the parking lot, I dimly saw the cluster of brick buildings that made up the complex. In front of my building, I recognized my own parking space — each resident had an assigned parking spot. There was another car parked in it. Suddenly and unaccountably, I was angry. The yellow car in my spot seemed to prove that everyone had decided I wasn't coming back. As we walked up the front steps, I ran my hand along the wall and remembered all the times I'd run up, hurrying to change clothes and leave for my aerobics class. I thought about Michael walking up to meet me, and how happy our times together had been. I didn't want to see him now — I didn't want him to see *me*. My mother unlocked the door, and I followed her, stepping into my living room. After more than a year, everything was still the same — the blue plaid couch, and the dark wood tables at either end, the warm blur of color over the couch, which must be my watercolor of flowers. I had bought that painting and another at an art sale in Poughkeepsie. Although I'd cleaned before I left, there was dust everywhere; I could feel it under my fingers as I ran them over the table in the breakfast nook. The refrigerator was empty, except for ice cubes and a box of baking soda. I wandered through the rooms a little, thinking about what I might take home with me. There seemed to be nothing really; it all belonged to this place, and not to the life I had in Pittsburgh. In the kitchen I found my one and only cookbook, actually a folder for recipes I'd clipped from magazines and saved. I never really enjoyed cooking, and I did very little of it, but I collected interesting "quick-fix recipes" to try occasionally. As I flipped through the pages, I could hardly read the titles.

As we tried to relax, I thought about how far off my recovery seemed, even after all this time. I still intended to keep my apartment open and ready for me to move in again, but that goal seemed even farther away.

For the first time since my accident, I considered a future radically different from the one I had planned. That future seemed to stare back at me, a huge void and emptiness; a shocking revelation. With my health gone and my intellect impaired, I was left empty-handed and rootless. I was scared. How would I support myself? What could I do with my life? For the first time, I felt really alone, really directionless.

I once heard a story: A man looks into an abyss, and finds nothing staring back at him. At that moment, the man finds his character, and that is what keeps him from jumping into the abyss. I thought this image was quite profound when I first heard it. It underlined the personal strength I applauded; it exemplified the self-sufficiency and the refusal to back down that I thought every person should develop. I always thought that the strongest people were the ones who clearly defined just what they wanted and then went after it. For me, that abyss appeared in the slow, disjointed time after I moved home from Harmarville. What I eventually found was not my character — I had been clinging to that for some time — but the realization that true strength comes from recognition of one's reliance on God, not the world, not the self, for all one's needs. True strength is derived from the acknowledgement that there is a Higher Power who stands ready to give guidance and direction — if one is willing to allow Him. Only God knows what is best for us, what it is that we lack and need above all.

I never thought I would say these words, let alone write them for so many others to read. Indeed, there was a time when I would have been embarrassed to know that others would scrutinize my words, especially words that reflect such personal conviction. In faith, in acknowledging the presence of God in one's life, however, there is no room for pride.

But this knowledge wasn't mine as I wandered through my apartment that evening. Later I went into the bedroom and went through the nightstand next to my bed, looking for my passport. I think, even at that time, I was idly thinking about going to Medjugorie. I found it among some scarves and silk ties, and right next to it was the small square white purse that held the pearl rosary I had bought in Jerusalem. Surprised, I took it out and strung the chain across my fingers. It was very light, and the pearl beads felt smooth and cool. My rosary was the last thing I expected to find. While I cherished all my travel experiences,

I had really forgotten about buying the rosary. I certainly hadn't used it since I came home. When I was in a coma, my parents told me, they had sprinkled Holy Water, saved from the vials I had brought back from Jerusalem, over me. I had really forgotten about them too. It seemed funny that the prayer beads should turn up at that point in my life. I took both the passport and the rosary home with me. I still felt sad and aimless, but I was aware of the suggestions God seemed to be offering me.

Just as I was becoming more intrigued with the apparitions in Medjugorje, my grandmother fell and broke her hip. While visiting her one day in the hospital, I told her what I knew about Medjugorje. She listened intently, and I found myself urging her to pray to the Blessed Mother, to ask Mary to intercede with Her Son. Mary could seek help for my grandmother in her pain and fear. Even as I spoke, I was astonished at my own words. I couldn't really pray or believe for myself, and yet here I was offering her this apparition of the Blessed Mother as a source of hope and consolation. She responded with hope and timid excitement, and I felt a great sense of peace come over us both. Although I sounded quite excited and firm in what I said to her, even to my own ears, I knew in my heart I was not totally convinced that the apparitions were real. I wanted to believe they were of God, but I kept asking myself, "Why would She be appearing now?"

A week or two passed, and my grandmother received a visit from a priest of her parish, who came to give her communion in the hospital. They had a conversation about Medjugorje and my grandmother told him about my interest in it. He said he had a video tape I might like to see, and he promised to bring it to her on his next visit.

When my parents and I visited her again a few weeks later, we picked up the tape, a documentary made by a gentleman named Kaminski. I took it home, anxious to watch it. That evening we sat in front of the television, mesmerized by its story. As the narrator related the history of Medjugorje, the tape showed scenes from the village and footage of the young visionaries as they experienced the apparition. It also showed close-up shots of their faces during the apparition, and if I sat very close to the television set, I could see them. I noticed that when the visions apparently began, their eyes moved quickly to a common point and focused there, where they apparently saw the Mother of God before them. The film was exciting and moving, and I watched it repeatedly, becoming more certain of the events occurring in Medjugorje.

According to the video tape and the newsletter published by Wayne Weible, the Blessed Mother told the visionaries that She would confide ten secrets that dealt with the future of the world, as well as the personal life of each of them. Once a visionary had received all ten secrets, the apparitions ceased occurring on a daily basis for that person. The older visionaries, Mirjana and Ivanka, no longer saw the Blessed Mother daily. The remaining four, Vicka (pronounced Vis-ka), Maria, Ivan, and Jakov, had each received nine. As of March, 1988, the four visionaries who continued to see the Blessed Mother daily had only one more secret to be revealed to them, and then the apparitions would end.

One point stood out in my mind: The Blessed Mother reportedly said that these were Her last apparitions on earth. I wasn't sure what this meant, but the idea left me uneasy and questioning. The words seemed to hold such finality and urgency. At the end of the video, there was a phone number through which additional tapes and further information was available.

Medjugorje seemed to promise so much; I wanted to know more about it. Impulsively, I called and ordered my own copy of the video. I reached the author, Stan Kaminski, and in the course of our conversation, I told him about my accident and my residual handicaps, noting, as always my visual problems. Mr. Kaminski heartily encouraged me to go to Medjugorje, and he told me of a woman from Pennsylvania who conducted pilgrimages to Medjugorje and who was fluent in the native Croatian language. I was surprised that he would offer me her name, and even more surprised that she was located so close to my home.

He said she was very well known by the people in Medjugorje and that she knew the visionaries personally. As I hung up the phone, I knew that I wanted to travel to Medjugorje, and that Helen Sarcevic was the woman I wanted to make that pilgrimage with. I called her immediately.

I was impressed by Helen's calm and quiet manner as she listened to my story. When I finished, she said, quite emphatically, that I should go to Medjugorje. I explained that my mother would come as well and help me with my personal needs. We spoke for a while about accommodations in the villagers' homes, and she told me that during our stay we would live with a family, and they would provide breakfast and dinner as well as a place to sleep and bathe. Helen explained that all activities in Medjugorje centered around St. James Church; the evening Croatian Rosary and Mass were the central daily activity in the village. The Rosary was said before Mass, and the apparition took place in the choir loft of the church promptly at 6:40 each evening. Only two of the visionaries, Ivan and Maria, went to the church each evening. Another, Vicka, saw the Blessed Mother in her room at her home each evening. The youngest, Jakov, also saw Her privately each evening; he was quite shy, according to Helen, and he shunned all publicity. As the video noted, Mirjana and Ivanka, two of the visionaries, no longer received daily visitations. Helen seemed quite knowledgeable about the events in Medjugorje, and I was drawn to her matter-of-fact conversation.

Unfortunately, as encouraging as she was in our initial conversation, Helen told me she had no openings for any of her pilgrimages until October of 1988. As more people learned about Medjugorje, her tours quickly filled up, and there were few cancellations. She promised to keep our names, in case any openings appeared before October, but she cautioned that cancellations were unlikely; once a person committed a deposit, they seldom gave up the trip. I hung up the phone and said disappointedly to Mom, "Well, I guess we'll just have to wait until October."

In the meantime, I tried to learn more about the apparitions and the events surrounding them. When my own copy of Stan Kaminski's video arrived, I invited Sister Agnes and Father Bob, the pastor of our parish, to watch it with me. After we had attended Rita Klaus' talk, Sister Agnes and I had begun to talk a little, and slowly we became friends. She was like no other nun I'd ever known, but, of course, most of my experience was based on the teachers I'd had in school. Essentially I had a child's picture, based on a child's memory, and she quickly offered me a new idea of what a woman of God can be. Sister Agnes herself is stocky, with broad shoulders, and she seems strong enough to take on all the burdens brought to her in her role as parish counselor. She has grey hair, blue eyes and a bubbly laugh. She's an astute listener, quick to detect sincerity — or a lack of it — in people's voices, and quick to respond accordingly. In conversation, she's very direct, and her acerbic humor often startled and shocked me. As we grew to know each other, to trust and care for each other enough to argue (something we often ended up doing), I felt an increasing trust and respect for her, and I shared my hopes about Medjugorje with her.

Of everything I heard about Medjugorje, nothing inspired more hope than the documented physical healings that people attributed to the intercession of the Blessed Mother. Everything I reviewed stated that physical healing — of many different afflictions and diseases — had been recorded and attributed to the apparitions. Cancer, deafness, multiple sclerosis, even blindness had been cured. Again, I thought I'd found a way to overcome my blindness. "It's happened for others," I thought, "maybe the Blessed Mother would ask Her Son to heal me, too." I wanted to see again; that was my sole goal in wanting to travel halfway around the world to a place I heard of only two and a half months earlier. My sister Jeanie often told me I was crazy, and sometimes I half believed her, but, just as I had once put faith in my low-vision therapy, I was willing to believe that going to Medjugorje would be a way to recover my sight.

I was at Harmarville for therapy about a week after I talked to Helen, and I went to their library to see what might be available to practice my reading. I was still determined to "prove them all wrong," to make myself see clearly and read alone once again. There were seven or eight large-print copies of Reader's Digest on the shelf. I was late for my next therapy, so I randomly picked up one, threw it in my bookbag with my log book, and hurried off.

That evening, after taking a shower, I sat down on my bedroom floor to dry my hair. As I was holding the blow-dryer, I spied my bookbag on the opposite side of the room and remembered the magazine. I pulled out the book, noticing the date — February, 1986 — for the first time. "Two years old," I thought, "how long do they keep these things?"

Then I tossed it onto my bed. It fell open to a picture of some children looking at a candle. The title of the article was "A Village Sees the Light." Something told me to read further, which was not an easy task; despite the large print, the words appeared jumbled together to me, and it was extremely difficult to focus on them. I began with the first sentence, piecing together each word slowly and deliberately. Finally, I thought I understood its content: "On a hot afternoon in June, 1981, two girls, Ivanka Ivankovic, 15, and Mirjana Dragicevic, 16, went for a walk outside the village of Medjugorje, Yugoslavia." I stood up, with the book in my hand, and ran down the stairs to our family room, where my father sat.

"Dad," I shouted, excitedly, "This article is about Medjugorje!"

My father looked up from his newspaper, and said, rather skeptically, "No, it isn't."

"Yes it is" I said. "Read it — Read it!"

My father began reading out loud, and, indeed, the article was about the reported apparitions of the Blessed Mother in Medjugorje, Yugoslavia. I could barely believe the coincidence: Of all the books on the shelf in the Harmarville library, I picked up this one.

The article described the severe questioning by both church and police officials the young visionaries underwent, as well as the numerous medical and psychological tests they submitted to. All the tests concluded that the six visionaries who claimed to see the Blessed Mother were, in every other aspect, nothing but normal children. The article also stated that during the first week of the apparitions, hundreds of people witnessed the healing of a three-year-old boy who had been mute, deaf, and virtually paralyzed since birth. Since then, numerous other healings had been acknowledged as well.

The article closed by noting that the entire village of Medjugorje was transformed by the apparitions, as the people strove to live the messages of prayer, fasting, penance, conversion, and peace, the peace that comes only from reconciliation with God and with one another, as the Blessed Mother instructed in Her messages. The Blessed Mother asked these things of all people, not just the visionaries, for all people are Her children.

The article only whetted my appetite for more information about the apparitions, just as the tapes and Wayne Weible's newspapers had. It seemed inconceivable that I would have to wait until October to make a pilgrimage to Medjugorje.

In March of 1988, another coincidence occurred. I was speaking to a new friend, a man who lived in Poughkeepsie, New York. I met Tom Malone through Joe Hines, my personnel manager at IBM. After I moved back to Pittsburgh, I used to call Joe often. His comforting, calm manner gave me support when I felt anything but calm myself. One day, he told me about Tom Malone, who was about my age, and who had also suffered from vision loss. Tom's eyesight had gradually deteriorated as the result of

Retinitis Pigmentosis. He was almost totally blind. After only one phone conversation, Tom and I formed a comradeship. It was borne of our mutual despair and anger at what had been inflicted on us, as much as anything else. We also shared a common thread of hope, for we both believed in a compassionate God who we did not always understand, but who we tried to trust. Tom made a pilgrimage to Lourdes each year, where the Blessed Mother appeared in 1858. As I learned more about Medjugorje, I decided to call Tom one evening and asked if he had ever heard about the place, and I was taken aback by his reply.

He was surprised that I asked him about Medjugorje; he had only recently heard about it, and he had called an office of the Catholic Diocese in Poughkeepsie to ask for further information. The office referred him to a Franciscan priest in Pittsburgh, Father Vincent Cvitkovic, who had been to Medjugorje many times. He was of Croatian background himself, and he was known by both the villagers and the visionaries in Medjugorje. Tom had called Father Vincent, and, in the course of the conversation, my name came up. When Father Vincent learned that I was living with my parents in the Pittsburgh area, he told Tom that "I practically lived in his backyard," and that I might give him a call, if I liked. He wanted to invite me to the Marian prayer meeting held each Friday evening at his church, Holy Trinity, in Ambridge, a small town about forty minutes from my parents' home.

Doubtful and hesitant, I finally made that phone call in early March of 1988. I didn't know what to expect from a "prayer" meeting, and, in another way, I was a little ashamed that I had been "reduced" to this level. Before the accident, attending a prayer meeting would have been the farthest thing from my mind, and the fact that I now considered this one made me examine myself a little scornfully. I thought, "How far will you stoop, Joan? Haven't you suffered enough humiliation yet?" Father Vincent listened as I went through my fears about my handicaps, my anger, and my confusion about why God had allowed this terrible thing to happen to me, and he responded to me with empathy. He was willing to allow a total stranger to vent all her frustrations to him, and I was impressed by that. When I finished, he said, "You will see things you would never have seen before the accident." He spoke simply, and with a self-assurance I didn't feel. I told him that I wanted to attend the Marian prayer service that Friday. Then my father spoke with him briefly, getting directions to the church.

I remember my first visit to Ambridge vividly. I was attracted to this small church; its beauty was reflected in its simplicity. On the wall above the altar was a lovely stained-glass window which seemed to draw my gaze upward and hold it there as the Rosary was recited.

The meeting was modeled on what occurred in Medjugorje each evening: we recite the fifteen decades of the Rosary, then celebrated Mass. During the Homily, Father Vincent expounded on the messages of the Blessed Mother, inviting us, as She had, to live Her messages daily, to strive for reconciliation, and to grow in holiness. Years had passed since I had said all fifteen decades of the Rosary in one prayer session. I had even forgotten some of the mysteries, but that evening I joined the others, reciting as well as I could each of the Joyful, the Sorrowful, and the Glorious Mysteries. At that first meeting, I felt I was meant to be there, participating in that worship, and I felt compelled to learn all the Mysteries by heart and to learn more about the rosary itself. I remembered the teachings of the nuns, who had always stressed the importance of the rosary to us. Like so many others, I put away "those beads" once I left school, and I hadn't used them to pray since I had graduated from high school. Now, at 31, I found the rosary and began to pray once again.

After Mass, the members of the prayer group met downstairs in the church hall for coffee and company. I didn't feel much like socializing. Sitting at a table quietly, while my father went to get coffee, I felt awkward, and aware that I couldn't see about this room as everyone else could. I think most people have experienced that vague isolation and self-consciousness that overcomes a new person among a group, but to feel this and be unable to see those others, to be unable to scan their faces for curiosity or responsiveness and thus unable to begin making your place among them, is worse.

Suddenly Father Vincent was at my side, kneeling down to speak to me. "Would you like to introduce yourself to the group, and share your story with them?"

I looked at him with surprise and genuine fear. "Oh, no, Father. I can't stand up in front of a group of people without seeing them. Please don't ask me to do this. I used to give presentations at IBM, but I can't get up in front of people now." I felt my heart racing, and I knew tears would follow momentarily. I never thought he would ask me to do such a thing.

Seeing my fear, he simply said not to worry, that no one was forced to do anything they might not want to do. He squeezed my hand and walked away.

I turned to my father. "Dad, I just couldn't."

The hall began to clear about twenty minutes later, and, despite my embarrassment at turning Father Vincent down, I knew I'd come again. Something at this Marian prayer meeting beckoned me to return. I didn't know exactly what, but I sensed that I belonged here.

A few weeks passed, and as we attended the meetings on Friday evenings, I started to get acquainted with a few people, and I didn't feel as isolated as I had initially. Even the Rosary became more meaningful as I learned and meditated upon the various Mysteries. Always I had the same feeling of rightness and belonging when I was in that church.

In late March of 1988, Helen Sarcevic called. I was at Harmarville in therapy, and Mom answered the phone. Helen said she had two unexpected openings for her pilgrimage to Medjugorje, planned for April 16th through the 24th. "Would the two of you like to go?" she asked.

My mother told her I wasn't at home, but that she would have me call as soon as I returned. When I finally got home, she told me about Helen's call. I said, "Well, you told her we would go, didn't you?"

Although she knew how much I wanted to go to Medjugorje, Mom thought it best for me to tell Helen myself. However much I resented some of the small tasks she took over to help me, I realized that she was sensitive to my need to feel independent. I think she also sensed that something important was about to take place in my life, and that I needed to move toward that change — and toward God — myself.

I called Helen to confirm our plans. She explained that we would need visas from the Yugoslav consulate office in Pittsburgh. Since we both already had passports, obtaining a visa was a simple matter. We would make our own flight arrangements to JFK airport in New York, where we would meet Helen and her daughter, Miriam. Helen wouldn't fly with us to the first stop in Dubrovnik, but she would meet the group a few days later in Medjugorje. Miriam would guide us from New York to Dubrovnik and accompany the group on the three hour bus ride from Dubrovnik to Medjugorje. She would also help the members of our group get situated in the various homes of the villagers.

The conversation flowed freely between us, with my mother throwing in her own questions. Again I was struck by Helen's ease and confidence with herself and her work; it was hard to believe we were talking about the appearance of the Blessed Mother in 1988! Clearly there was no question in her mind concerning the validity of the apparitions. I hung up the phone feeling sure that she was the best possible guide for our first pilgrimage.

After talking to Helen, I said to my mother, "Wouldn't it be wonderful if I could make an anonymous donation to our church, so that Sister Agnes could come with us?"

By then we had become close friends, and I knew how much she dreamed of going to Medjugorje one day. After all, it was really her invitation to hear Rita Klaus and Wayne Weible speak, just a few weeks earlier, that had really introduced me to Medjugorje. I wanted very much for Sister Agnes to make this journey with me.

Mom said, "Yes, that would be wonderful, but don't you think she'd know who made that anonymous donation?"

I shrugged my shoulders and picked up the phone.

I meant to matter-of-factly set about arranging for her to go with me, but Sister Agnes, who was in the church rectory, answered the phone, and I couldn't hold back my news. I started shouting into the receiver, "Sister Agnes! Guess where I'm going!" She didn't even have a chance to answer. "I'm going to Medjugorje!"

She was silent for a few minutes. Then she said, "Joan — When are you going? Who are you going with? What dates will you be over there?"

I answered her just as tersely: "Helen Sarcevic of Mir-Peace Tours. Mom and I are going on her pilgrimage, April 16th to the 24th." I wondered why she was bogging me down in all these details, when I was already trying to work how I might persuade her to go.

Again she was silent for a bit. Then she said "Are you sitting down?"

She sounded so hesitant and formal. "Yes, I am, Sister," I said.

"Guess where I'm going with Father Bob, and Alvy and Kenny, from our church?"

I knew the answer. I whispered, "Medjugorje?"

"Yes" she said, a little defiantly. "We're going with a group that leaves Chicago on the 18th of April."

We both sat there, stunned, as the news slowly sank in.

Finally, she said, "Do you realize we're going to be over there at the same time?"

I thought of my exchange with Mom, only a few minutes ago. Wouldn't it be nice if I could make an anonymous donation to our church, so that Sister Agnes could go with us? Many times, when I was feeling despondent, especially about how little control I had over my circumstances, Sister Agnes would say, "Maybe God is trying to show you who the true Director of Traffic really is." Despite the long string of coincidences and serendipitous connections that had brought me to this moment, I hadn't realized that all the planning for this trip had been taken out of my hands from the beginning. As I said goodbye to Sister Agnes, I considered the things I'd learned and done in the last weeks. How evident God's role seemed as I looked back.

I called Father Vincent to tell him I was going. He gave me very specific instructions, and he said I would have a chance to visit the visionary Vicka at her home, as all the tour groups did. He told me to ask Helen to translate my story, and to listen carefully to whatever Vicka said to me. She was, after all, a woman who conversed with the Blessed Mother daily; her words could reflect instruction that the Blessed Mother wanted me to hear. Father Vincent made no promises, but I wanted to meet with Vicka. Struck with the path my life had taken so far, and inspired by the possibilities that might await me in Medjugorje, I set out with my mother, excited, hopeful, and sure I was doing the right thing.

Belief in the events of Medjugorje is a matter of faith, and faith is a gift, rather than something to be explained. Some things, I was learning, must be accepted in faith alone. I felt I truly believed in all that was occurring there.

I knew that the apparitions were best judged on the fruits they bore, and, according to everything I'd heard, these fruits seemed good and healthful. Millions of people were said to have converted there, returning to church, receiving the Sacraments and embracing God once again. I heard nothing that contradicted Church teachings — on the contrary, everything the Blessed Mother asked of people reflected what Her Son had taught during His three-year ministry on earth. I knew I must make a conscious decision to center my everyday life on prayer, penance, fasting, conversion, and peace through reconciliation with God and with man.

But first, I thought, I needed to get over the hurdle imposed by my limited eyesight. I planned to ask for a physical healing in Medjugorje; once healed, I could live the Blessed Mother's messages to their fullest. Although I was re-examining my relationship with God, I based my faith on a precondition: In effect, I told God that if He would restore my eyesight, I would do whatever He wanted. I should have known better; I had always been taught that faith must be unconditional.

When I thought of the people I'd learned about, people like Rita Klaus and Wayne Weible, whose lives had been totally changed because they embraced the messages of the Blessed Mother, I knew their lives had been changed dramatically and permanently. As I prayed the Rosary again, attended Mass frequently, and fasted on Wednesdays and Fridays in accordance with Her requests, I told myself I had been converted. But in my heart, I was uncertain about changing my life so that it revolved around God, so that it centered on what He wanted rather than on the pursuit of my own desires. I knew the Blessed Mother's messages frequently stated that one must abandon one's self to God totally, but I wasn't ready for that.

My trip to Medjugorje was a means to an end: to receive a gift of physical healing and to see clearly once again. I also wanted to witness for myself just what was going on in Medjugorje before I gave myself up to it — to God — utterly. I didn't question that the Mother of God truly appeared; somehow, I knew in my heart that She did, but I did harbor doubts about whether She would help me directly. She knew very well how long I had been away from my faith. Perhaps She would see me as a hypocrite, turning to Her only in my time of great need. The Bible was very clear on what Christ had to say about hypocrites. She might despise my petition, rightfully questioning just how firm my faith really was. All these things ran through my mind as I prepared for that pilgrimage. I didn't want to be a hypocrite, but I needed help, and I did believe that Her Son could heal me. Although I knew I wasn't worthy of such a gift, I felt compelled to go and ask. I had finally reached a point where I had to trust in someone other than myself and my doctors, and I needed to sustain my faith, no matter how lukewarm, with the possibility that I might receive a gift of physical healing. "Surely it couldn't hurt"; I thought, "and this might be the only way for me to recover my vision."

It's incredible that I was still trying to put God on my schedule, drafting in a time to be healed. Still in the infant stages of my spiritual recovery, I thought it possible to prescribe the results I wanted with only cursory regard for God's will. Even as I tried to move His hand to my will, God worked in me, through me, in spite of me. There is a saying in Medjugorje: "All who go to Medjugorje are invited." It is the Blessed Mother who does the inviting. Looking back on the way everything was "arranged" so that I might make my first pilgrimage, I see Her hand in everything that occurred. As I prepared for the trip and made my plans, I tried to imagine what I might find in Medjugorje, and what might happen there. I wanted to do something, to somehow arrive there prepared for the gift I wanted, and my renewed striving for prayer and reconciliation seemed insufficient. I wanted to take my own gift, and I decided to choose one for Vicka, the visionary I hoped to meet. One day I went into a shop, and the counter was covered with music boxes of all kinds. I went through, winding each one up and listening to their varied music until I found one that played "How Great Thou Art." I listened to the steady clear notes and hummed the melody with it. "This is it," I thought, "this is the right gift." Before we left, I decided to keep a journal of my trip. For some time, I occasionally felt that I ought to be writing about my life, that I ought to record and work through everything I had experienced since that day of change, December 2, 1986. Sometimes I said to myself, "You ought to be writing about this, Joan. Not too many people have gone through what you have in the past 14 months. Somehow, you should get this down on paper." Then some other part of me responded with: "You're crazy. You can't even see clearly, or read your own printing. How could you ever hope to accomplish such a feat? You're dreaming, kid, you're dreaming." Perhaps I was, but the dream kept presenting itself.

Usually I put the idea away, too overwhelmed by the difficulties I had in reading or writing to seriously consider it, but I expected this visit to Medjugorje to be something special, something significant, and I was prompted to try and record as much of it as I could. Every evening I dictated an entry, and my mother wrote it out for me.

We left for Medjugorje, Yugoslavia on April 16, 1988. Our journey started off well, when we were unexpectedly bumped up to first class on the flight from Pittsburgh to New York. I stretched out my legs and leaned back in the wide seat, feeling the stewardesses swish back and forth past me. I was too excited to sleep or read. I thought about all the other flights I'd made, flying to Denver or heading out of the country for IBM, or just for my own pleasure. My mother had worked as a ticket agent for United Airlines, so Jeanie and I had enjoyed free flights throughout our childhood. We had traveled to Hawaii several times. Remembering those times, both of us excited and intent on the Pacific Ocean and tans, joking with each other and coming together as only sisters can, I smiled. I wished Jeanie saw Medjugorje as I did, and for a moment I wished her there into the seat beside me.

At JFK airport, Mom and I stopped at the Pan Am Clipper Club room, which brought back many bittersweet memories for me. I had spent plenty of time in this room, waiting for flights to countries in Latin and South America and the Far East as part of my work. I still sorely missed that life, and I wondered if I would ever stop yearning for it.

We met Helen Sarcevic at the ticket counter. Some of the other members of our group — Francis and Bernie, and two young boys traveling with a Brother Anthony were there as well. Helen assured me that we would go to Vicka's house; I was determined to follow Father Vincent's instructions to the letter. I wanted to give her the music box, and I wanted to ask her to play it for the blessed Mother when She appeared to Vicka in her room.

I was going to Medjugorje with my list of wants in hand, and at the top was recovering my eyesight. I had so much to learn, and Medjugorje proved an unlikely but compassionate training ground. I had been called to Medjugorje by Mary, but what I actually found there was Her Son. There I reacquainted myself with Christ and His teachings, and I gained an understanding of what I could and would do for Him — not just what He could do for me.

We arrived in Dubrovnik early Sunday afternoon, April 17th. The airport was small and drab, but outside it was a beautiful, sunny day, and very warm. Miriam, Helen's daughter, who acted as our guide until Helen arrived a few days later, met us there. We took a bus to the Excelsior Hotel in Dubrovnik, then called Dad to let him know we had arrived safely. Over dinner, we met Jean and Christine, another mother/daughter couple from Pennsylvania, who were making their second pilgrimage to Medjugorje. I discussed my injury with them, and Christine said, "Now I have something to pray for."

The next day, after breakfast, we readied our things, then walked around the city for most of the morning. My mother's parents are Slovak and Croation, and she had grown up hearing them speak a language very similar to the one that we heard now. She told me that she recognized a little of what was spoken around us in the shops. Then we rejoined the group at the hotel, where we all boarded the bus to Medjugorje.

The landscape changed considerably as we drove out of the city. The small cars and low grey buildings gave way to fields and rough cement roads. Most of the people are farmers, working small fields of tobacco and vegetables. Women, their faces lined by the wind and the sun, worked side by side with men in the fields. They wore long black dresses and colorful kerchiefs.

Warm weather comes very early there; in April, the temperature was about 70, and as the summer approaches, the countryside gets much hotter and much more humid. The village itself is located in the middle of a group of small, rocky hills. From the bus stop, we could see a few small shops, and, farther back, the simple sturdy houses of the villagers, and behind those, the steep hillsides. The church wasn't visible. The bus dropped us near Anna and Antonio Jerovich's home, where we stayed during the week. Anna welcomed us and gave Jean, Christine, Mom, and me rooms on the second floor. Our room overlooked the church and Mount Krizevac (Cross Mountain).

I was amazed by the whole village. Anna and her husband, like most other families in the village, had accepted strangers into their homes for the past seven years simply because the Blessed Mother asked it of them. Every year, more and more people came to pray, hopeful of having their prayers and their lives fulfilled in some way, and the people of Medjugorje offered them food and a place to stay as a matter of course; their hospitality was a part of their lives, which were already busy and hard. Each morning, I woke up to the sounds of their lives: to a rooster crowing in the yard and the sound of the church bells, calling people to Mass. As we walked to St. James each morning, we often shared the roadside with sheep or a cow.

Every morning, Anna gave us breakfast, which was thick brown bread that she baked herself, fruit, juice, and fiercely black coffee, for those who could drink it. Mom and I brought tea bags with us, as Helen had suggested.

That first evening we went to Mass at St. James Church. The huge sanctuary was crowded, and there were no empty seats, so we stood during the Rosary and Mass. Later I learned that the church was built by the villagers, and that it seated 1600 people, even though the village itself included only about 300 families. The villagers said they hadn't planned for such a massive structure, but as they worked they were compelled to build the church larger and larger. The service was in Croatian, and the sound of it was beau-

117

tiful. I had feared the unfamiliar language would be a barrier, but the Church seemed filled with the meditative holiness I had come to associate with the Rosary.

Mother and I decided we would walk back to the Jerovich's, but we got lost in the unfamiliar village streets. We flagged a taxi and eventually made it home, late for dinner. Afterwards we set out for Apparition Hill, the site of the Blessed Mother's first apparition on June 24, 1981.

The visionary Ivan and the youth prayer group to which he belonged met most Monday evenings on the Hill, where the Blessed Mother often appeared to them, sometimes giving a message to Ivan for all gathered there as well as the parish. Only Ivan actually saw the Blessed Mother when She appeared, but there was a joy in just being aware that you were present in Her wake, and I hoped fervently that She knew I was there. Under the incredibly bright and close stars, people sang and prayed in many different tongues. Again I felt I was right to be there. The next evening, two young girls who were members of the same prayer group came to visit us, and they confirmed that the Blessed Mother did appear to Ivan at the meeting we attended. We were grateful and happy just to have shared the experience.

The following day — Tuesday the 19th — I finally met Vicka. We attended an English Mass in the late morning, then our group went to Vicka's home. Miriam pointed to my mother and me and asked Vicka if she could see us sometime, and she agreed, asking us to return the next day at 9:00 a.m. I was elated.

We spent the rest of afternoon browsing through the shops, which offered an array of rosaries and other religious items. I had promised to buy rosaries for several friends, and I spent plenty of time choosing them. Later, we went to St. James Church for the Rosary and evening Mass.

On Wednesday morning something extraordinary happened. As we were dressing, Jean came into our bedroom and asked Mom to come to the upstairs balcony where she could see Mount Krizevac clearly. I stayed in the bedroom, knowing I couldn't see whatever it was Jean wanted to show my mother. I heard her direct Mom's attention toward the site of the giant cement cross which the villagers had built in 1933. She asked Mom to look at Krizevac and describe what she saw.

A few moments of silence passed, then I heard my mother exclaim, "The Cross is gone! The Cross is gone!"

I jumped to my feet and ran to the balcony. "What do you mean, 'the Cross is gone?' That's impossible. How can that cement Cross be gone? It must weigh tons."

Then Jean gently asked, "Do you see anything else, Rita?' Mom was silent for a few moments, and then gasped, "Oh my God, I see a figure of a woman . . . It's Her! It's the Blessed Mother!" Mom just stood there with her mouth open, rubbing her eyes, and staring at the top of Cross Mountain. Only, now, she said, the Cross had disappeared, and in its place was a figure of a woman, which she immediately identified as the Blessed Mother.

Jean asked gently, "Can you describe what you see to me, Rita?"

Slowly, Mom said, "I see a ghost-like figure of a woman, all in white, and she's turning, as though the wind is blowing her. The Cross is not there, but in its place is this figure of a woman."

"I'm so glad you said that, because I saw, and I still see, the same thing," Jean said. "I thought I was imagining it."

When we went downstairs and told Anna what they had seen, she was brusquely accepting. "Ah — Gospa" was all she said. "Gospa" is Croatian for "Blessed Mother."

Our breakfast was shorter that morning. Through the visionaries, the Blessed Mother had asked that all those who are able should fast on bread and water twice a week, on Wednesdays and Fridays. That morning, we'd eaten only a slice or two of Anna's homemade bread, which was cut so thick and seemed so hearty that I wasn't hungry afterwards.

Miriam took us to Vicka's house promptly at 9:00. We carried petitions from home — the prayers of people unable to make this trip — a picture of myself and a picture of Michele, a young friend I met at Harmarville. I also carried my gift to Vicka.

When we arrived, Vicka invited us into her house, which surprised all of us. Her room was very simple, with a huge statue of the Blessed Mother in one corner, and a small crucifix and a picture of Christ's face hanging on the wall.

I gave Vicka a note from Father Vincent, written in Croatian. Vicka smiled as she recognized his name. I told my story to her, and Miriam translated. When Miriam finished, Vicka looked intently at me. Then she said something to me in Croatian; Miriam again translated: "Vicka says that God has given you this cross, Joan, because He loves you, and because He wants something from you, something that only you can give Him. She says that you should continue to pray much and fast much, and most importantly, you must believe."

I asked if Vicka would take my photographs and place them on her altar in her room, and she readily accepted both pictures. I also gave her the music box and asked if she would play it for the Blessed Mother when She appeared to her each evening. Then we left. We felt very blessed and privileged to have spent time alone with her.

At the English Mass on Thursday, we finally came across Sister Agnes, Father Bob and Sister Alfonsus. I had been expecting them for several days. After hugging one another and sharing some of our initial experiences, Sister Alfonsus took me aside and said God had given me this cross in order to strengthen me. I was struck by how similar her words were to Vicka's. While I found myself drawn to this very warm and gentle woman, inside I was confused. Hadn't I been strong enough before the accident? Not too many people could have undergone what I had and lived to tell about it — was I not strong now? I felt that more than strengthening, I needed healing.

Early in the afternoon we boarded a bus that took us to see Father Jozo, who was the parish priest of St. James when the apparitions first began. Although he initially hadn't believed the visionaries, he was soon convinced that their experiences and their faith were genuine. He was imprisoned for eighteen months because he refused to say that they were hallucinating or lying about the apparitions. Ultimately the Yugoslavian government forced him to leave Medjugorje, and he lived and preached in another parish about forty-five minutes away.

When we arrived at Father Jozo's church, St. Elijah's, he spoke to us. He wasn't tall — about 5'10" — and he had brown hair and brown eyes. Many said he had the most penetrating gaze, and a beautiful smile which revealed white, perfect teeth. He also had a scar above one eye, a reminder of his imprisonment.

As he spoke, Helen acted as translator for everyone gathered there. He talked of the importance of prayer and fasting, and he emphasized praying with an open, receptive heart. He spoke for over an hour and a half, and nothing but his voice and Helen's echo sounded in the church. All faces were turned to him, and I tried to picture him in my mind.

After his talk, Helen arranged for our group to meet Father Jozo in the courtyard outside the church. Miriam called my mother and me aside, and she told Father Jozo about my accident. Then he prayed fervently over me, placing his hands at the back of my head, directly over the occipital area. I wondered how he knew this was the source of my problems, and I thought, "Miriam must have described my injury to him." We thanked Father Jozo and left, feeling we had both experienced something very special and very comforting. There was something wonderful and inexplicable about this simple and quiet man; he exuded a gentleness and peacefulness I had never seen before. I couldn't help wishing some of that peace would rub off on me. Helen remarked to us later that this blessing was better than being in the choir loft at the time of the apparition. I wasn't sure what she meant by that.

On Friday, April 22, after the morning Mass, we met Father Rupcic, a Franciscan priest living in Medjugorje.

He spoke of his original distrust of the apparitions, and he described his growing belief, as he has witnessed the many conversions and the physical healings that had been documented — there had been 340 documented healings at that time. He also blessed me before we left.

Afterward we walked up Apparition Hill again, and there Mom and I met Sister Agnes and Father Bob. As we all hiked up the stony trail together, I was struck by the new and mysterious patterns so clearly working in my life. There we were, approaching this holy place with the two people who had come to visit and pray over me while I lay in coma in the initial days following my accident. Like my parents, I believed that Father Bob and Sister Agnes were instruments of God, used to awaken me. Sister Agnes had asked for the intercession of the Blessed Mother, and I felt sure it was her prayer that led to my awakening. Now we all climbed together, and I reflected on a life almost lost, and on the people and events that had changed me so. I wanted my sight back, and I prayed for it as I walked, but I also understood that something else, some other desire and progress filled me as well. More than ever, I was aware that it was Mary who had brought us together here. Mary led us all to Medjugorje, and I was convinced She would lead me back to Her Son.

We took a few pictures, including one of me placing my left hand, which had very limited feeling, on the small blue cross that marked the spot where the Blessed Mother first appeared. As I reached out to place my left hand on the cross, I suddenly said, "God forgive the man who did this to me."

My mother looked at me, startled and surprised. "Joanie, what made you say that?"

In a way, I was as surprised as she was, and I had to think for a minute before I could answer her. "I don't know, Mom, it just seemed the right thing to say. I kept thinking the entire time we were walking up this hill, 'How can I be on this sacred hill, begging and pleading with my Mother to intercede for me to Her Son and ask Him to restore my eyesight, while I still carry this hatred in my heart towards the man who did this to me — the man who caused my accident.' It's not right that I ask Her for help, if I can't forgive that man. I'm OK, Mom." I felt God inspired those words; He made me see my error.

From that day on, the hatred, the ugliness, the cursing I had uttered against that man was gone. I was free from all the hostility I had carried in my heart for his sake. In Medjugorje, I found myself not only able to forgive him, but able to begin praying for him.

Soon we walked down the hill, and I returned to the church to go to confession. There I saw Father Phillip, a man I'd met briefly the day before when I gave him the letter Father Vincent had sent him. Father Philip recognized me from the description in Father Vincent's letter. He said Father Vincent had asked him to read the letter to me, but at the moment he didn't have it with him. We talked a while, and he said my life had been spared for a reason, and that God would reveal His reason to me in His own time, not mine. Listening to him, I felt I must pray for patience.

On Saturday we visited Vicka's house again. Referring to the photographs I had given Vicka to place on her altar, Helen asked if there was a message for me. Vicka said only that she had "recommended me to the Blessed Mother." I was disappointed, but I knew I had enjoyed many privileges already, visiting her room and sharing my story with her privately. If a specific message from the Blessed Mother was ever meant for me, I knew that I would be made aware of it somehow.

Later that day, I met Father Bob at the foot of Mount Krizevac and journeyed with him up the hill, stopping at the Stations of the Cross that had been placed there by the villagers years earlier. It takes three hours to walk up to the cross and down again, and most pilgrims see it as an act of penance and patience. Everyone climbs and descends by the same path, and climbers often must pause, waiting patiently for others to go by. Our walk was deliberate and meditative, and the rocks of the path were worn smooth by the daily travel.

Once we arrived at the top, where the huge cement cross stands, Father Bob said healing prayers over me. I seemed surrounded by a network of support and loving prayer in this place, and that evening, as we walked down to the village, ready to go to the evening Rosary and Mass in St. James Church, I realized this was our last night in Medjugorje. My mother and I had experienced so many special blessings in the short time we had been there. When I planned my trip, I had no idea it would be this difficult to leave. I was almost overwhelmed with a desire to stay, but I knew it wasn't possible. I was increasingly certain that my work, some task I hadn't identified yet, waited for me. I consoled myself with the knowledge that I would return to Medjugorje one day. After Mass the priests conducted a healing service, and they blessed the religious articles that many people had bought in the village and brought to this last service with them. The whole evening seemed like a fitting farewell.

The next day, a Sunday, we woke at 6:30 and said goodby to our hosts. Anna gave us a lovely wicker basket my mother had admired several days earlier. In return, we left our towels, sheets, a pair of jeans and pajamas — all hard items to come by in Communist Yugoslavia.

We took the bus back to Dubrovnik and boarded a flight for Amsterdam. There was some mechanical difficulty with our plane, and we didn't actually leave the ground until 11:00 that evening. We arrived in Amsterdam at 2:00 a.m. on Monday morning, went directly to the Golden Tulip Hotel, and fell into bed.

By 8:15 the next morning, we were up again and preparing to leave Amsterdam for New York. As we flew back, I thought about our trip out, and all the things I had planned and hoped for. I knew my life had changed again in this short week — I could feel it — but I knew that much depended on me; I must return home and start living the messages given by the Blessed Mother in

Medjugorje. Conversion, after all, meant change, and I prayed that God would continue to work that change within me. As I thought about my desires and things I had prayed for on my way to Yugoslavia, I realized that those had changed as well. Now I felt I could pray for spiritual change, for patience and faith and the courage to let God dictate those changes, rather than only begging to have my old life restored. I wasn't returning physically changed or healed; I was still legally blind, and I still had very limited use of my left hand. But a spiritual healing that I could only dimly sense was growing within me, sparked by my experiences there, calling me to a closer relationship with God. I returned home with a new sense of hope, a desire to know God better, and the intention to be open to whatever His plan was for me. I realized that I had to trust in Him, and let Him lead. I knew it would not be easy to relinquish control over my life to Him, but in Medjugorje I had promised to try.

Something had occurred in Medjugorje. I went in answer to Mary's invitation, but there I found Her Son as well, and I found myself wanting to know Him better. I also felt that there was something more for me to do, something more than simply living the Blessed Mother's messages.

As it is for all pilgrims to Medjugorje, it was important that I return home and be active in my faith, a faith rekindled by my experiences there. I came home to Pittsburgh uncertain of what awaited me. I kept thinking of Vicka's words — that God had given me this cross because He wanted something from me, something only I could give Him. What did she mean? What did I have that only I could give? I prayed that I would be led to understand the meaning of these words.

I went again to the Marian prayer meeting the Friday after we returned home. As we knelt reciting the Rosary, I was aware that my concentration on the mysteries was greater, more focused. I wasn't just following the words; instead I could meditate upon the lives of Christ and Mary as I prayed. As I meditated on the Sorrowful Mysteries, it occurred to me that Christ and Mary had been human, too. They had suffered, and they understood my suffering. This realization comforted me as nothing else had. "They understand," I repeated to myself. I asked God to help me trust in Him, as He wanted me to do.

As always, the group assembled in the hall after Mass. As my dad and I sat at a table, Father Vincent came over and asked if I would be willing to share my experiences in Medjugorje with the group. I looked at him, remembering how I had nervously rejected his first invitation a few months ago. I had lost my confidence when I lost my vision, and it was hard to believe that once I had stood in front of all levels of IBM management giving presentations.

This time I knew I couldn't refuse. I thought, "If you believe in the events occurring in Medjugorje as firmly as you claim to, then you better stand up and share your experiences."

Later my dad told me that I looked at Father Vincent, squared my shoulders and said, "Yes, I'll speak." At the sound of my "Yes," my dad said, he uttered a sigh of relief, and a silent prayer of thanks. He felt I might finally break out of my shell, might give up my self-imposed exile, which I had so often justified by saying that I didn't want to share my pain with others, that people had their own pain and sufferings, and they didn't need to share mine. But if acknowledging the sufferings of Christ and Mary could help me bear my own and trust in their compassion, there must be something in such sharing.

There would be no more hiding, no more taking comfort in the fact that I could just blend in with all the others, drawing no attention to myself. I understood that God wanted me to do something for Him, and I knew I must respond positively. Somehow, I knew He would give me the courage to accept Father Vincent's invitation.

I stood up in front of those people in Ambridge — almost a hundred of them — knowing I must look awkward, as Father Vincent positioned me in front of the group, and I could feel my heart racing. I began speaking slowly, still doubting that I was actually going to do this. I remember telling the audience that they would have to excuse me, that I didn't see very well. Then I told my story.

I told them I was originally from Pittsburgh, but that after college and graduate school, I had moved to Poughkeepsie, New York, to pursue a career with IBM World Trade Corporation. I spoke briefly about my rise within the company, and how my future appeared to be "horizons unlimited." I told them I had truly lived a dream, traveling around the world, assuming increasing responsibility. And then I spoke of how that dream suddenly came to a halt as I became the victim of a hit-and-run accident on December 2, 1986. It was the first time I had ever spoken publicly about the horrors of that time, my battle for life, and the doctors' words to my family: "All you can do now is pray." I told them of the circumstances that ended my coma eighteen days after the accident, and about my struggle at Harmarville. I related how my parents had been told that my leg was so badly broken I would probably walk with a cane, and I pointed out that I had walked to the front of the room freely. I told them that my worst nightmare came true, for I couldn't see clearly, couldn't focus my eyes on the things around me. Again the doctors had said I would never see clearly again.

I spoke of my anger at God, and my despair at the thought that He had allowed this to happen to me. I thought that God hated me, and that He was ignoring me in my despair. But, as I told the people that night, unknown to me, God heard all my anguish and my anger. He would answer me, but in His time and His way, not mine.

I described how I had been led to Medjugorje, and my experiences there. I told of my meeting with Vicka, and her words to me, and that I was uncertain of their meaning. I finished by thanking them for allowing me to share so much with them.

Father Vincent walked me back to my seat, and I sat down, relieved, but unsure that I had made any sense at all. I remember that he hugged me. I vaguely heard people

127

clapping, but I didn't quite understand that it was a response to my words. I just thought they were being polite. Once at my seat, I was unprepared for the onslaught of people who rushed up to me to thank me for sharing my story.

There was so much going through my mind: What exactly had I said that moved these people to come and hug me, and express such heart-filled emotion? Some were in tears. I truly didn't believe that my story was all that remarkable. After all, I made no claims to actually having seen the Blessed Mother. I was still struggling; I was still rejecting my cross. "Surely, these people could see that. Surely, their applause was out of sympathy for my plight," I thought. I had gone to Medjugorje, not to be convinced that the Mother of God truly appeared there, and certainly not to convince anyone else that She had, but with the hope that I might receive a physical healing. This was no saint who told her story; this was a struggling Christian, a woman in search of hope.

In the months ahead, I came to understand the meaning of Vicka's words. I needed to learn to trust in God, and in time I would see how God worked His plan through me and in me, often in spite of me. Slowly I learned that God moves the heart of a person to do His will. I had much to learn, but I was finally on my way.

After that first talk at Ambridge, an entirely new facet of my life opened up in a way I could not have imagined. As a result of that evening, I was invited to speak to other groups of people at various churches around Pittsburgh, sharing with them my story and my experiences in Medjugorje. I never knew when an invitation to share would come my way, but in time I learned that they were not extended by chance — I learned that nothing happened by chance. At first I resisted some invitations, still caught up in my pride, still fearing others' perceptions of me. I struggled to set aside my pride, marveling at the various ways people and invitations came to me, and I learned to trust that God would never send me out to fail. I never sought out places to speak, but they kept appearing.

As I gained confidence, my delivery became stronger, and my sharing became less a story of Joan and her experiences, and more a story of the miracle that was unfolding in Medjugorje. I knew, in my heart, that I was to spread the message of Medjugorje through my own personal witness. In Medjugorje, as I watched the villagers accept the major changes the apparitions wrought in their lives, as they made it their duty to host the people who came, I learned the importance of obedience. For the past seven years, they had opened their homes to total strangers every day because the Blessed Mother asked it of them. I knew I had to try to be that selfless in my own awkward struggle to obey. In time, I understood that obedience is the cornerstone of faith, and that it is one of the greatest gifts a person can give to God. At 31 I had to learn to be obedient to my faith, and obedient to the teachings of it, all over again. No longer could I fashion a do-it-yourself type of religion; I had to abide by Church teachings and adjust my life accordingly, which was no small task. Yet this is what the Blessed Mother asked, and this is what I strove to do. God and His Mother were tireless in their efforts to assist me on my journey in faith.

Whenever I spoke, I always shared Vicka's words with my listeners. They still perplexed me; although I knew my witnessing was in response to God's plan, I felt there must be something else, something about Vicka's words I was missing. As I said earlier, sometimes I thought about writing down all that had transpired in my life since the accident, and occasionally I discussed the idea with my parents. I thought that writing might provide a type of healing for me, as I vented all the emotions that were raging through my mind and body in response to the circumstances heaped upon me. Still I held back, bemoaning my awkward writing abilities and lamenting, "Even if I tried it, what would I call it? My Greatest Challenge?" My parents made no response.

On a June morning in 1988, I awoke and went down to the breakfast table, where Mom and Dad sat finishing their meal. As I sat down, I said, "I'm going to write my story, and I'm going to call it A Greater Vision." My parents just looked at me, but I was as astonished as they were. Finally my father said, "Wow! Where did that come from?"

"I don't know," I said, "but it's so beautiful, it's so simple, it's so perfect. A Greater Vision. That's what I am to call it."

I spent the next few weeks diligently printing on bold-line paper, beginning with the Introduction and Chapter One, "Personal Background." By mid-July, I had begun Chapter Two, "The Accident." At first, the words came to me easily, as if the whole story already existed inside my head. It felt good to be working at a large project again, and to be working at something I could do myself. But my visual problems were always a hindrance, both physically and emotionally.

On July 27th, I reached a crisis of confidence and spirit, and it was answered. That afternoon I sat at the kitchen table, struggling to read my own rough printing. I was home alone; about fifteen minutes earlier my father had gone to pick my mother up from work. I decided to review what I had written on Chapter Two, and so far I'd gotten through only three of the nine or ten pages I'd written. It was too difficult. Even though I printed (rather than writing cursive), and even with the help of my line guide, all the letters appeared jumbled together, so that it was nearly impossible for me to read my own printing. I felt tears of frustration begin to sting my eyes, then stream down my face, and I sobbed. "Can't You see how hard this is for me? Don't You want me to do this?" I was yelling at God again. "I don't even know if I'm doing the right thing, if I'm supposed to do this, at all."

I cried for several minutes before I could gain control of myself again. I realized that my parents would be home any moment, and I didn't want them to find me in tears. I ran up to my bedroom and got my rosary out of the nightstand drawer where I kept it, and I began saying a few prayers to help me calm down.

Unused as it had been for so many years, it seemed ironic that this rosary, the one I bought in Jerusalem, the one I found in my nightstand in Poughkeepsie and carried to Medjugorje, was the first thing I reached for now. Only months earlier, I wouldn't have thought to reach for it. I began saying the prayers, and I had gone through only a few "Hail Mary's" when the phone rang.

I ran downstairs, the rosary dangling from my hand, hoping to catch the caller. It was my friend, Jae, calling from Connecticut to tell me she'd received the package I sent her, a VCR tape and literature about Medjugorje. Jae was excitedly asking me questions about my trip there, and she wanted to know if, and when, I planned to go again. I told her I had no immediate plans to return, but that I would like to very much.

We talked several more minutes about Medjugorje before Jae interrupted, saying "Joanie, I can tell that you've been crying. I can hear it in your voice. What's wrong?"

I told her how frustrating my attempts to read my own printing were. "I've got to be crazy to think I can do something as taxing as writing a book, when I can't even read my own printing," I said. "Who am I, to even think that God, Himself, inspired this, and wants me to do it? Who am I kidding, to think that I am supposed to undertake such an impossible feat? I must be crazy, Jae," I said woefully. With that, I began to cry again. Jae simply listened and did her best to console.

As she managed to change the subject to a less emotional topic — her work, I happened to glance down at the rosary, still in my hand. "My, that chain looks gold," I said to myself. But I felt I couldn't rely on my own eyesight, and I said nothing to Jae. "It's your imagination, Joan," I said to myself. But I continued to look closely at the chain while Jae talked about some problems she was having at work.

About five minutes later, my parents came home. As my mother walked up the cellar steps and into our kitchen,

I waved my rosary at her. She looked at me quizzically, then took the rosary from my hand and walked over to the sliding glass door that led to the outside deck. I had mouthed the words, "It's Jae," and kept listening. My mother walked into the kitchen again, after looking at my rosary in the bright sunlight. She was nodding her head, confirming that my rosary chain, once silver, was now a golden color. I stopped Jae in the middle of a sentence, saying, "Jae! You're not going to believe what just happened. My rosary chain turned gold! The chain was silver, and now it's a golden color."

I could hear Jae gasp at the other end of the line, and I tried to explain how rosary chains were reportedly turning golden in many areas of the world. I told Jae what the meaning of this outward sign was, according to the interpretations I had heard. Many people said that the changing rosary chains were the Blessed Mother's call to prayer, a sign not of individual faith or holiness, but of the world's need for these things.

I told her that I never thought it would happen to me. I was crying again, as I said, "Jae, do you understand what happened? I had been upset about not being able to read my own printing, and questioning whether I was right in struggling to go on with this writing. I was searching for confirmation, beginning to doubt whether I was doing the right thing. I think I just got my answer."

From that day, I no longer questioned whether I was doing the "right" thing. As I continued writing in the months ahead, I came to understand the meaning of Vicka's words: God gave me this cross because He loved me, and because He wanted something from me — something that only I could give Him. Only I could give Him my story, for only I had lived it. While there was definite healing for me in the words I struggled to put down on paper, the inspiration and the ability to rise above the fear and humiliation as I reviewed the words I wrote for all to read and judge could have only come from God. He spared my life so that I could do this, and he receives all the glory. I am only the instrument.

CHAPTER SEVEN

MEDJUGORJE REVISITED

I RETURNED TO MEDJUGORJE in October of 1988. It is difficult to explain why I felt so compelled to return after only six months, but, then, I knew I would go back to Medjugorje even as I flew home from my first pilgrimage there. This second time, I went with no idea of what might await me. I only knew that I felt strongly compelled to return, this time with both of my parents. I was eager to share this experience with my father, especially, since he had shared so much of my therapy and pain with me. We traveled as a family, minus one, but we carried my sister Jeanie in our hearts.

Two weeks before we departed, I was in Ambridge, at the prayer service I attended faithfully each week. After Mass, the group gathered in the church hall for the customary social get-together. While I sat drinking a cup of coffee, a young boy named Patrick ran over to me with his "Garfield" doll, a stuffed copy of that smug cartoon cat. I thought, "Sixty people down here, and he singles me out to play with him." As I talked with him, I found myself looking at him intently, concentrating on his face. Always before, he had been nothing more than a blur as he ran from table to table in the hall. Now, as he calmly stood before me, I could finally take him in, at my own pace. As I looked into his face and touched his golden-colored hair, I remember thinking, "What a beautiful boy you are, Patrick." We played a few more minutes before he took off again.

As my father and I drove home that night, I couldn't stop talking about Patrick, and as I climbed into bed that evening my thoughts were still on him. I lay awake for close to half an hour, thinking about how receptive and innocent he seemed, and I realized that I no longer knew how to be the same way. When had I stopped trusting, when had I stopped being capable of awe? My own life seemed so complicated. When had it become such a huge burden? Perhaps I'd made it that way myself, tried to exert my control over too much. I realized I had too often made a choice for Joan, with little regard, if not outright ignorance, of what God wanted for me. I used to think I was capable of directing so much, and I found that I really controlled very little. Somehow, as I lay awake in my bed that evening, I knew everything I had ever done wrong in my life, and I was filled with remorse and disgust for all the times I had hurt God. I began to cry, pushing my sobs into my pillow so my parents wouldn't hear them. I must have cried for twenty minutes, before I cried out, "Oh Mother, I am so sorry." Immediately my room was filled with a beautiful, sweet aroma of roses. It was so overwhelming, so strong, that I thought I was in the middle of a rose garden. I lay there stunned. I remembered being at Vicka's house in Medjugorje, standing in the small court-yard in front of her home, and hearing someone in the crowd say, "Can you smell the roses? Do you smell the roses?" I hadn't understood what these people were talking about. I looked at my mother and said, rather skepti-cally, "Do you smell roses? I don't. Do you?"

My mother shook her head. "I don't smell roses, at all, Joan."

Finally, still lying there with my face in my pillow, I simply uttered, "Oh, you're here." The aroma of roses lasted for only two or three minutes, and I wondered if I had imagined it. I lay in my bed, motionless, astounded by what I had just experienced.

Our tour guide, Helen Sarcevic, had said that the scent of roses signified the presence of The Blessed Mother. I never forgot that. And now, almost six months after my first trip to Medjugorje, the scent of roses filled my own room. I didn't sleep the rest of the night; I was too excited by the experience.

The next morning I ran down to the breakfast table, anxious to tell Mom and Dad about last night. Only my mother was home, and she sat at the kitchen table eating her breakfast. I said, "Mom, you're not going to believe what happened to me last night. I'm so excited and so amazed — I don't think I slept at all." Then I told her about the roses.

My mother listened intently, allowing me to finish, before she said, "Joanie, I know what you are saying. I've smelled them too."

"You have?" I was incredulous. "When?"

She said that sometimes, while she was putting clothes in my drawers or changing the sheets of my bed, she had noticed the smell of roses in my room. She never mentioned it to either Dad or me because she thought she was imagining it.

I was glad I'd shared my own experience with her; it helped her realize that her own experiences weren't just her imagination. She too remembered standing outside of Vicka's house while people asked one another about the roses in the air. It was amazing to think that we both had this experience in our own home, far away from the special holiness I associated with Medjugorje.

"Wait until we tell your father!" my mother said excitedly. "He'll be so surprised." She shook her head. "I wonder if he'll believe us."

When dad came home, my mother said, "Joanie has something to tell you."

I related the whole story again, telling him about my sadness, the smell of the roses in my room, and what Helen had said.

When I finished, Mom told her story. Then we both sat back, waiting to see what he would say.

He didn't say anything for several minutes. Instead he just looked from me to her. Finally, he spoke: "Well, I know what you are talking about, because I've smelled the roses, too. A few weeks ago when I was laying the new tile in the upstairs bathroom, I suddenly felt tired. So I went across the hall into Joan's bedroom to lie down on her bed for a few minutes to rest and take a break. After only a few minutes, I was startled by this overwhelming aroma of roses. It was so strong, I felt as though I was in the middle of a rose garden. Then it went away, and I knelt down at your bed, Joan, and said a prayer of thanks."

We all looked from one to another, amazed that we had all been blessed with such an experience, and yet kept it from each other out of doubt, or out of fear that the others would think we had let our imaginations run wild. Sharing our experience only convinced us all that the Blessed Mother was closer than we thought.

On Friday, October 21, 1988, I went to the Marian prayer service in Ambridge, as usual, but that meeting seemed particularly special, a beautiful and apropos preparation for my second pilgrimage to Medjugorje. My parents and I were leaving the next afternoon. Home again after the meeting, I was excited, anticipating our departure on the next day. As I climbed into bed, exhausted but unable to relax and sleep, I thought of all the things I still had to do before leaving. I had to finish packing; I started worrying whether I had packed the correct clothing — this time of year Medjugorje would be much colder — whether I was taking enough money, whether our tickets were in order, whether the weather would be favorable, whether I would get to meet with Vicka and Father Jozo privately, as I had done in April. I could feel myself getting more and more tense, more and more upset. In the middle of my agitation and restlessness, a thought entered my mind clearly, overriding everything else: "Love your cross, daughter, for it has brought you closer to My Son, and, to me."

I lay still, struck to silence and a kind of peace. There was no doubt in my mind that Mary was sending me this thought. My holy Mother spoke directly and matter-of-factly, but She soothed and comforted as well. I was calm;

my worry, and agitation had completely disappeared, and I was at peace. I knew in my heart that the Blessed Mother also meant to make me aware that this pilgrimage would be different. I was going to give thanks — not to plead or make demands of God. Rather than trying to shape Medjugorje into a particular experience for me, this time I would go with an open heart, praying to be thankful for whatever my Lord and His Mother wanted to show me. I would pray to accept whatever God had planned for me. There would be no demands, this time; I would go expecting nothing, doing my best to thank God and praise Him for all the graces He had already given me.

The next day we were at JFK airport in New York again, where we joined our group and Helen Sarcevic. We all boarded the flight to Dubrovnik, where we would spend the night, together. Helen had arranged for Mom, Dad and me to take a taxi to Medjugorje early the following morning. We were anxious to get to Medjugorje, and Mom and I had already toured Dubrovnik in April. The rest of our group planned to spend Monday in Dubrovnik.

Again I was excited to be returning to Medjugorje, this time with both parents. It seemed that I understood so much more about what took place in Medjugorje than I did six months earlier, at the time of my first trip. Then my heart was not open to God's plans; I came only with my list of demands, looked only for physical healing. Only a quick fulfillment of my own needs mattered to me. Sitting on this second flight out to Yugoslavia, I felt different: not as angry, not as hopeless. I still felt that this pilgrimage was special for some reason I didn't yet know. I sensed it when I prayed, and for once I was willing to be patient.

That evening, in Dubrovnik, our group gathered together in St. Blaze Church for Mass. Father Don Rinfret, who was from Baltimore, was acting as our spiritual director, and he said Mass. The gospel he read that evening was Mark 10:46-52, which told of Christ healing a blind man. I felt as if this message had been chosen for me.

Jesus asks the blind man what He might do for him.

"I want to see, Lord" was the man's response.

Jesus then asks the man if he firmly believed that He could do this for him.

The man replied, "Yes, Lord," and his sight was restored. The Gospel seemed a blessing, a gift from God. I cried as I listened to it, and I think my parents did too. Later Father Don told me that many other people in our group were crying as well. He also told me that when he first read the passage before Mass, he immediately thought of me. I guess others in our group had the same thoughts. I wasn't aware that the others knew of my visual handicap; obviously word had spread through the group. At one time, I would have been embarrassed, and angry that all those people knew of my vulnerability. This time, I was struck by their concern, and I felt surrounded by the hopes and love of many people.

After Mass, Father Don asked me if I wanted to take a walk around the streets of Dubrovnik and talk. I think he sensed how moved I was by the Gospel that evening. Until we talked, I had no idea that he was so very moved as well.

We walked along the streets for over an hour. I told him about my accident, and about how I was led to Medjugorje, first in April, and now again in October. After relating many of my experiences since my accident, I told him that there were no coincidences in my life anymore. I was beginning to believe that everything happened for a reason, all in accordance with God's plan. He seemed very interested in what I had to say, and I was so happy to share my thoughts with him. I felt I'd found a friend for life.

The next morning we packed and climbed into the taxi, which had been sent by Stanko, the owner of the residence where we planned to stay. During the three-hour drive to Medjugorje, I found myself thinking repeatedly, "I'm coming, Mother, I'm coming."

Our rooms at Stanko's were simple and comfortable, and our bath was attached to the bedroom. As in April, hot water was limited, a thing to be conserved and shared carefully. This residence was larger, and Stanko offered housing to several other pilgrims as well. Usually we all ate together, sharing hot, heavy meals of pork or chicken, stuffed cabbage, some vegetable from the household's garden, and brown bread.

When we went to St. James Church for the evening Rosary and Mass, the church was as crowded as ever. We could see many women from the village kneeling on the floor, praying fervently during the Rosary and the Croatian Mass. We could see flashbulbs going off, aimed at the choir loft, where the Blessed Mother appeared to Ivan and Maria each evening at 6:40.

The next morning, Tuesday, we went to the English Mass at ten. The gospel read was about the wedding feast at Canaan. Wishing to spare the young couple from embarrassment, Mary alerted Jesus to the fact there was no more wine. When She told Him this, He replied, "Woman, My time has not yet come." To which Mary replied by telling the wine servers, "Do whatever He tells you" (St. John 2:9). Jesus performed His first public miracle by changing the water into wine at the wedding feast in Canaan.

In the reading, two points were very clear to me: First, Jesus performed His first public miracle at His Mother's invitation, thus underlining the importance of Her intercession; the Mother made a request, and Jesus the Son complied — Why would Her intercession not be a powerful one? Secondly, if God, the Almighty Father, chose Her from all women to be the Mother of His Son, and charged Her with the responsibility of raising His Son, why had I refused for so long to see the power of Her intercession? I had ignored Her requests, ignored whatever Her Son had told me to do in the Scriptures. Somehow, I had chosen to push aside twelve years of schooling which stressed the teachings of Christ in favor of a life governed only by my rules and the rules of the world.

That evening, my spiritual blindness was abundantly clear to me, and I was appalled by my ignorance. I cried that evening during the Mass, in sorrow and shame, painfully aware of my ignorance towards the Mother of Christ, acknowledging that She had never ignored me.

After Mass, hiking with the other members of our group, we climbed Apparition Hill again, for the second time that day, and we met several other young people that evening as well. I led the Rosary for all present, reciting the Sorrowful Mysteries. When I finished, the wind suddenly kicked up. There had been no breeze during our climb up the hill, nor during our recitation of the Rosary. I remembered Helen telling our group, days earlier, that Mary had told the visionaries that She was always present in the wind.

Wednesday morning, on our way to English Mass, we passed a small gift shop at the bottom of the hill near Stanko's. Mom suggested we stop inside. We stepped into the tiny shop, which was really no larger than a bathroom. My mother was looking at the rosaries on display when I spotted a picture leaning against the back wall.

I vaguely saw what appeared to be a painting of the Blessed Mother, but all I could make out clearly was Her head, which was encircled with a crown of stars. "The Madonna of Medjugorje!" I thought. I continued to stare at the face, and the shopkeeper came over to where I stood and watched me squint at the painting. Suddenly he moved forward and dragged away a bookcase that actually covered much of the painting. There was the Madonna: She wore a white veil, a gray dress, and that magnificent crown of stars. In the bottom right-hand corner there was a singular steeple, evidently representing one tower of St. James Church. In the opposite corner was a small cross, the one atop Mt. Krizevac. It took time for me to focus on all these details, and I found my gaze always returning to the face of the Madonna. "How beautiful She is," I said aloud to Mom, and she, too, stared at the painting. I asked the shopkeeper its price. I couldn't really say why; it wasn't a personal gift, or something to buy for one's self and keep at home; it needed to be displayed in a place where many people could see it. I knew that without question. It was also more expensive than I had hoped, and I hesitated, then told the shopkeeper I would return the next day.

Mom and I returned to St. James Church to join the rest of our group. Helen had arranged for Father Rupcic, a Croatian priest, to speak with us outside the Church. Father told us that as of that date (October 26, 1988), there had been 341 documented physical healings of various afflictions and diseases, both of people who had come to Medjugorje, and of those who had begun to practice the Madonna's directives in their lives. Father Rupcic held a huge book, a record of all the documented physical healings and medical reports. He leafed through it, then stopped to read an account to us. "Here" he said, "is a story of a woman from the United States, who was cured of multiple sclerosis, without ever having come to Medjugorje.

My parents and I looked at one another; we knew who she was before he mentioned the name.

"You may know of her. Her name is Rita Klaus."

Rita Klaus! I couldn't believe that of all the healings he might have mentioned, Father Rupcic had chosen the woman I had met.

Later that afternoon, Dad and I went to hear Father Philip speak at St. James Church. During his talk, he said, "If God, the Almighty, chose Mary, of all women, to be the Mother of His Son, why do we question Her role in God's plan? Why do we think, given this role, that She would not intercede for us to Her Son, and that Her intercession would not be a powerful one?" He told us that Mary had been sent to Medjugorje by God the Father, to call us all back to His Son. "It is up to us to respond to Her call. Will we?"

The next morning, before breakfast, we met a group of Italians who were also staying at Stanko's. After Mom told them that I couldn't see, they insisted on praying over me. Only one person, Vincent, spoke any English. They prayed over me in Italian for at least 15 minutes, then they rushed off to catch their bus, heading to St. James Church for the Italian Mass. Vincent and a couple other people returned, gave me a huge picture of the Sacred Heart of Jesus and some Italian prayer books, then ran off again.

We had our breakfast in peace, then Helen took our group to Vicka's house. Helen asked Vicka to pray over me and a few others in our group who had special needs. Vicka remembered me, and she led Mom, Dad and me into her bedroom. She prayed over me for about ten minutes, keeping one hand on my head and the other hand on my mother. With Helen interpreting, I told Vicka I had a gift for her, another music box, but I hadn't brought it with me that morning. Helen would bring it by later that day. Vicka smiled and nodded her head. I think she remembered that I brought her a music box last April. This time, I had chosen one that played "Silent Night" — appropriate, I thought, for the up-coming Christmas season. As with the first music box, I asked Vicka to play it for the Blessed Mother when She appeared in her room.

On Friday, the Italians met us at breakfast again, and they invited us to meet them for prayer after dinner that evening. We went to English Mass, then met the rest of group outside St. James, where we boarded a bus which took us to Father Jozo's parish. I looked forward to hearing this very special man speak once again. I remembered how kind he had been to me last April, and I remembered his powerful blessing.

As we drove from one village to the next, I talked with my parents and listened to the other people talking around us. It felt good to be traveling with these people, meshing our spiritual journey with this physical one. It seemed to me that there were more people in Medjugorje this time; it seemed that the Blessed Mother was drawing more and more people to Her, and that more and more were answering Her call.

We arrived at Father Jozo's church in the early afternoon. As she had in April, Helen acted as interpreter for the audience in St. Elijah's. The church full of people was completely silent, and all focused on Father Jozo's voice.

After his talk, Helen took the three of us to Father Jozo's rectory for a personal blessing. Father Jozo prayed fervently over me for several minutes, placing his hands on the back of my head, just as he had done last April. When he was finished, Helen asked me if I had anything I would like to tell Father Jozo.

After a moment, I said, "Yes, tell him that I have been inspired to write my story, and to call it 'A Greater Vision'." Father Jozo stared at me for what seemed like several minutes, after Helen had translated my words for him. I stared directly back at him without blinking. It occurred to me that he was somehow "reading" me. I looked into his eyes, smiled, and nodded, trying to confirm that what I had told him was true, and that I was as surprised as anyone at the turn my life had taken.

Finally he broke eye contact with me, looked at Helen, and said something in Croatian. Helen said, "Father Jozo says that when your book is finished, your eyesight will be restored."

I gasped, and I felt my eyes fill with tears. I took Father Jozo's hand and said, "Thank you, thank you." My parents and I walked back to the bus, stunned. I never expected such a prophesy. My mother squeezed my hand and said, "Did you hear what he said to you?"

I just nodded, unable to say more.

My parents were quiet almost all the way back to Medjugorje. I meditated on Father Jozo's words, trying to take in their full impact slowly. I had started writing for myself; I knew it was healing for me in an emotional sense, and in a spiritual sense as well. But I had never imagined that it might result in a physical healing. I realized that I must simply tuck this prophesy from Father Jozo in the back of my mind, and just let it lay there. I wouldn't try to speed up my writing, or to rush to complete it, in order to fulfill his prophecy. One thing I was sure of, even then, was that my writing couldn't be completed one minute before its time, not one minute before God desired it done. And if a healing awaited me upon its completion, then that was in God's Hands, and I was not to question, but simply allow God's plan for me to be fulfilled.

That evening, as we had promised, we met with the Italians. They had asked for a separate room, so that they might pray over me in privacy, and they took Mom, Dad and me there. We had no idea what to expect, but when one of the men walked in carrying a portable heater, we should have known we were in for a long evening. We just looked at one another; these people were sincere in their devotion and their belief in God, and the interest they had shown in me, their concern over my handicaps, seemed genuine. But they were determined that my eyesight was to be restored that night, and they meant to pray until it happened!

Two and a half hours later, after many, many prayers in Italian, after two of the women lay prostrate on the floor, after my hands and body were ice-cold from the chilled room despite the heater, they were still going strong. My mother sat stiffly in a chair. Perhaps more than anyone, I knew how cold it was in the room, and how little toleration she had for the cold. I was tired, and hungry, but I didn't know how to politely tell them that we should leave, that we all needed some sleep, if nothing else. Finally, I did speak up, telling them it was time for all of us to go back to our rooms. I thanked them repeatedly for their efforts and their prayers, but I also told them that my eyesight would not be restored one moment before God wanted it so, and that they should pray rather for my patience.

As we started to leave, Vincent stopped me. He held several fingers up in front of my face, saying, "How many fingers am I holding up?" repeatedly, alternating the number in front of my face. By this time I was punchy, and I felt sure that I was too tired to answer him correctly — even if I could have seen them. We left exhausted, but charmed by the faith and determination of these people who reached out to surround me as if I were one of their own.

Saturday morning, we dragged ourselves out for breakfast, and there we said good-by to Tony, Vincent and the other Italians who had prayed over me last night. Tony brought me three miniature roses. Where he found roses at that time of year was beyond me — it must have been close to freezing that night, and the morning was still chilled. I hadn't really spoken to this man at all — he spoke next to no English, and most of the people in their group seemed content to let Vincent be their translator. Tony seemed a little older than me — perhaps in his early forties. He had thin, dark brown hair and very brown eyes. His voice was almost like a tenor, and he was a little soft around the middle. I laid the roses next to my teacup and I thanked him, which Vincent duly translated.

After we'd eaten, Mom, Dad and I went upstairs to get ready for the English Mass at 10:00. Almost immediately there was a knock at our door. My father answered it to find Tony standing there, alone, with another gift for me — a beautiful lead crystal framed picture of the Madonna of Medjugorje. I thanked him, and he became very emotional. I knew he wanted to tell me something that was obviously very important to him, but I couldn't understand his words. Finally, he left the room and quickly returned with one of the young girls who cleaned the rooms. She spoke some Italian and some English. Tony took my hand and began speaking rapidly in Italian. I still couldn't imagine what he was trying to say, but I could feel the emotion behind his words, and I could feel his intent gaze on my face.

The young girl looked at him, then at me. Then she said, in English, "He says he doesn't care if you cannot see. He says he loves you and wants to marry you."

I stood there with my mouth open, hardly able to believe what I had just heard. This man, someone I'd met only a few days ago, someone I wasn't capable of conversing with, was proposing marriage!

Behind me, my parents were struck still with astonishment, and I could almost hear them thinking, "Now what's she going to do?"

I looked at Tony and spoke to our amused translator: "Please tell him that I am very flattered by his affection towards me, but I cannot marry him. I have much work to do, in getting my life back in order. I do not want to hurt him, but I must be honest with him. I do not have the same feelings for him that he has for me." As the girl tried to translate, I wasn't sure how much she understood of what I was trying to say, much less how well Tony understood her translation.

He grasped my hand, said something more in Italian to me, then moved towards the door. I kissed him good-bye and thanked the girl for her help.

She just shrugged her shoulders and left.

I turned to my parents, who were both staring at me. "Can you believe that? Tony fell in love with me after only a few days!" I knew he was sincere in his feelings. I could sense that without question, but when he started to talk about me going to live with him and his "mama" in Italy, I didn't know how to say no without hurting his feelings. "I can't believe this happened," I said, "I just can't believe it."

Neither could my parents. We came to Medjugorje in search of spiritual renewal, and I got a marriage proposal in the process.

When I look back at that experience, I find it less un-settling, and more likely to make me smile. I had been unsure and nervous about my appearance for so long. For a time at Harmarville, I was sure that my face was horri-bly scarred, and that everyone was afraid to tell me so. Even after I proved to myself that my face looked as it always had, I still felt self-conscious, as if not seeing other people's faces meant that I had no control over my own. I feared that people approached me only out of pity, not because I had anything to offer. Maybe Tony's proposal was God's way of showing me that I was not as grotesque as I imagined myself; maybe he was a gentle attempt to make me feel attractive again.

My negative vision of myself prevented me — at least in part — from moving towards total conversion. I needed direction and a purpose in my life. Too often I still felt as though I ought to apologize for being alive, and for producing so little. My life, which seemed full of such direction and promise before my accident, seemed to have little of either at that time — at least no direction in which I could take pride. I had my writing, and I accepted invitations to share the story of my re-awakened faith, but something was still lacking. Although I portrayed myself as grateful that I was still alive, the truth was that I mourned my past life, and I was still angry that it was no longer mine. I was also conscious that God knew both my longing for the past and my lack of purpose.

I couldn't know then that God prepared for me a purpose greater than any I could have ever imagined. In His infinite wisdom, He knew I wasn't ready for such a revelation. There was much I still needed to learn about serving the Master rather than the servant.

Later that afternoon, as Mom and I walked towards St. James Church, Mom suddenly said she didn't feel well, and that she needed to sit down. I was concerned about her; we had kept up a hectic schedule from the moment we arrived in Medjugorje, and I thought the pace had finally taken its toll on her. We went into a small restaurant near the church and ordered a pizza. Only a few minutes after we had ordered, she suddenly said that she felt much better, and that we should hurry on to the church. We apologized to the waiter, telling him that we needed to leave quickly. I don't think he understood, but then neither did I.

"We have to get to the church," she insisted, "we have to get to the church."

As we approached St. James, we noticed a crowd gathered to the left of the church.

"What's going on, Mom?" I asked.

She looked at the crowd. Suddenly, she said, "That looks like Father Jozo, over there."

I shook my head. "That couldn't be, Mom. He's forbidden to step foot into Medjugorje by the government, isn't he?" My mother persisted, and as we walked closer she said, "It *is* him. It's Father Jozo."

I stared ahead, straining to see him myself. Finally, I caught a glimpse of a man in a dark brown robe, but I couldn't see his face.

Later, Mom told me, Father Jozo glanced up from the crowd, and his eyes rested directly on me. He walked away from the crowd, stood in front of me, looked straight into my eyes, pointed his finger, and said, "Book."

I just looked at him; I was dumbfounded that he remembered me and my book, but I was thrilled.

He laid his hand on my forehead and began to pray over me, as he had when our group visited his church earlier this week.

"What a grace, to have received two special blessings by this very special servant of God" I thought to myself.

Later that day, when we caught up with Helen, I related to her our chance meeting with Father Jozo. When I told her that I had thought the Yugoslavia government had forbidden him to return to Medjugorje, once he was released from prison, Helen said that he could enter Medjugorje, but he was forbidden to celebrate Mass within the village. She agreed that our meeting with Father Jozo could hardly be called chance — perhaps "grace" was a better word.

On Sunday, our group climbed Mt. Krizevac, hiking up to the huge cement cross and stopping to say the Stations of the Cross along the way. I thought of the villagers who had climbed this mountain many years, working to mark the fourteen Stations of the Cross along this rugged hill, carrying the cement up the sometimes treacherous mountain to erect the thirty foot-high cross at its apex. "Such great faith!" I said to myself, "such great faith." All forty-eight members of our group made it to the top, despite the fact that some were in poorer health and some had special obstacles to overcome. Mom, Dad and I lit four blessed candles and left them at the foot of the Cross.

After we walked down again, on the way to our village house, we stopped once again at the small shop to look at the oil painting of the Madonna. Again I felt strongly that

I should buy it, but again I told the shopkeeper that I'd come back the next day.

Monday, October 31, was our last day in Medjugorje. I awoke with the overwhelming, inexplicable feeling that I need to go to confession. I had intended to go for the past few days, but with our hectic schedule, I hadn't yet made the time. "Poor excuse," I told myself.

After English Mass, the last Mass spoken in English we would attend on this pilgrimage, I stood outside the Church where confessions were heard all day, waiting my turn. The day was cold; the wind never stopped blowing, and the wall of the church did little to block it.

After hearing my confession, including all the anger and despair I continued to feel over the injustice of my accident, the priest said that the Blessed Mother wanted very much to use me in God's plan, and that She would. I told him about my writing, and he said that She was already using me.

All day long, I kept thinking about that painting of the Madonna. Something inside me kept repeating that I had to buy this painting, and a date, December 9th kept running through my head. I didn't understand what it stood for. "What's December 9th?" Suddenly, I knew. This year, on December 9, our church was holding a special Mass in honor of Our Lady of Medjugorje. I knew that this painting had to be there.

My parents went with me as I stopped again to see the shop-keeper and the painting. I told him that I very much wanted to buy the painting, but I hesitated at the high cost. In his scarce English, the shopkeeper explained that he couldn't go any lower in price because the painting was not his. He only acted as an agent for the artist, Coric Pero, who was from Mostar. Despite my hesitancy, I knew I couldn't let the price prevent me from buying this painting. I told the shopkeeper to wrap the painting for me. He had to strip the canvas from the frame and roll it up. As I counted the money out, he suddenly handed me back five dollars, indicating that he wanted to make this contribution towards the painting. He pointed to his own eyes, and he said that he too had eye problems. "Five operations" he said. For the first time, I noticed his very thick eyeglasses. He understood.

I kissed the man good-by, and with my parents hurried to St. James for the Rosary and Mass. We couldn't find a taxi, so we walked all the way to the church. I knew the Rosary had already started, and I was anxious to get into the Church, because I knew that Our Lady blessed all people and objects inside St. James Church at the time of Her apparition. I wanted Her to bless the new painting.

When we finally arrived, St. James was so crowded that we couldn't get inside the Church. We walked around the massive building three times, trying to find an entrance, but it seemed impossible.

On the fourth circuit, we found a small doorway. We were cold, and had almost given up hope of getting inside, but there in the alcove we were protected from the wind — there it was almost warm. Father Rupcic, the priest who had spoken to our group earlier in the week, approached and opened the door, allowing another priest and a man in a white robe to go inside. Then he locked the door and left.

We realized that this doorway led up to the choir loft where the two visionaries, Ivan and Maria, met each evening to witness the apparition.

"Mom," I said anxiously, "we have to get inside the Church. This is our last night, and we should be there for the apparition."

Still, none of us moved. The alcove was warm and inviting, and we already knew there was no other way in. And so we stayed a few moments more.

Suddenly, Father Rupcic reappeared. As he walked towards the door, my dad said, he seemed to be looking for something in particular.

As he approached the doorway near which we stood, my mother stepped out in front of him. "Father Rupcic," she called out to him. He turned around quickly, apparently surprised that someone would call him by name. My mother then said, in Slovak, which she learned to speak from my grandparents, "Please, my daughter cannot see."

Father Rupcic looked at her, and then at me. Then, in silence, he took the key out of his pocket and tried to unlock the door which had opened so easily only moments before.

I thought, "He can't open it. He's going to get frustrated, and just tell us to leave." My heart sank. Father Rupcic finally knelt down, inserted the key once again, and then we all heard the click of the lock sliding back. Father Rupcic opened the door, pushed my mother and me inside, and quickly locked the door behind us.

Still shocked by this sudden turn, we started up a dark, winding metal staircase. Above us were rafters. As we climbed, I tried to think of all the beautiful prayers I could say to the Blessed Mother, and I tried to keep in mind everyone I wanted to recommend to Her. At the top, was a door with a panel of yellow, opaque glass, too cloudy to see through.

Suddenly the visionary Ivan stuck his head around the glass and looked at us. His look clearly said, "What are you doing here?"

Again, my mother repeated her Slovak and added, "Father Rupcic, Father Rupcic."

Ivan looked at me intently, and quietly opened the door that led to the choir loft.

As we walked across the cement floor to two empty chairs — the only ones left, as if they waited for us to arrive, we could hear the prayers of the Rosary rising up from the sanctuary of the church below. Already seated were the priest and a man dressed in white who, we learned later, was a bishop from the committee investigating the apparitions. There were also two men with video cameras, and two or three others, present, I guessed, because they had special needs, like myself.

I noticed a beautiful oil painting of the Madonna on the wall in front of us. It was the size of the painting I had bought that day, but its colors were much deeper, more brilliant.

Ivan and Maria entered the room. I took my mother's hand. My heart beat so strongly, I felt sure that everyone in the choir loft could hear it. Ivan and Maria walked across the room and knelt in front of the painting. Ivan was directly in front of Mom, and Maria directly in front of me. I realized that The Blessed Mother was going to appear in front of them, and that Mom and I would be only inches away from Her. Ivan and Maria began reciting some prayers in Croatian. Then, abruptly, they were both quiet. Maria nodded her head, as though she was saying "yes." Later Mom said that Ivan's and Maria's lips moved, but no sound could be heard coming from their mouths. It was just as I had seen in the Kaminski tape. I couldn't believe that I was privileged enough to be present during this blessed moment.

I had always thought that if I were actually allowed to witness an apparition, I would say these beautiful prayers to the Blessed Mother, that I would tell Her all the people I wished to carry in my heart to Her and to Her Son, begging and pleading for their intentions. Instead, the moment I realized that She was standing in front of me, only inches away, I dissolved into tears. All my prayers, so carefully prepared in my mind, were gone. I found myself saying repeatedly, "I'm sorry, I'm sorry" and "I'm here, I'm here." In the few minutes I knelt in the choir loft with both my earthly and my heavenly Mothers, I became a small child aware of everything I had ever done wrong. I knelt there sorrowfully and tearfully, pleading for forgiveness from Her Son. I never thought it would be like this; I had conjured up in my mind an image of myself standing before Her with dignity and a firm upper lip, beautifully laying out in front of my Mother all my needs.

I should have known that one can't plan one's response to the love and graciousness of Christ and His Mother, and that they did not expect such things. They continue to pour out their love and mercy on the world and God's children, regardless of their sins. If Their love is so great, how could I begin to comprehend the love of God, the Father. Although I began to realize the two great examples God had given the world through His Son and the Mother of His Son, I still had much to learn about God's love and His infinite mercy. That was, after all, what Medjugorje was all about — a call to holiness, nothing less. There in the choir loft, I knew that my response to this call had to be nothing less than an affirmative, unquestioning, "yes." Unlike the Blessed Mother's, my "yes" had been a long, long time coming, and I knew I still had much work to do.

When the apparition was over, Ivan and Maria blessed themselves, stood up, and left the choir loft. Mom and I walked down the stairs that led to the body of the Church and attended Mass, a fitting way to praise God and thank Him for the gracious blessing He had given us that evening. Our hearts were overflowing with love of God and His Mother. Quite suddenly, a thought occurred to me. I leaned over and whispered to my mother. "Mom, I think this was Our Lady's way of thanking me for buying the oil painting, before we came to church."

My mother just looked at me, smiled, and hugged me. Somehow, I knew that my heavenly Mother was smiling at me, too. I embraced Her in my heart with a "thank you" that filled my entire being. Whenever I recite the prayer, "The Magnificat," (St. Luke 1:46-54) I reflect back upon my few minutes in the choir loft, and pray that, like the Blessed Mother, my soul too might "magnify the Lord."

PART THREE

"There is a certain kind of humility in hell which is one of the worst things in hell and which is infinitely far from the humility of the saints, which is peace. The false humility of hell is an unending, burning shame at the inescapable stigma of our sins. The sins of the damned are felt by them as vesture of intolerable insults from which they cannot escape. Nessus shirts that burn them up for ever and which they can never throw off.

"The anguish of this self-knowledge is inescapable even on earth, as long as there is any self-love in us: because it is pride that feeds the burning of shame. Only when all pride, all self-love has been consumed in our souls by the love of God, are we delivered from the thing which is the subject of those torments. It is only when we have lost all love of our selves for our own sakes that our past sins cease to give us any cause for suffering or for the anguish of shame."

— Thomas Merton

CHAPTER EIGHT

TOTAL ABANDONMENT TO GOD: A RECKONING

THIS SHORT CHAPTER, while presented here, was not written until some time after the last chapter of this book was written. I thought, and others thought, "Well, the book is finished. Enjoy the feelings that come with the completion of a huge, long-standing project that had spanned more than three years." But something nagged at me and ached me, a sense that something had been left unfinished, left unsaid. I buried this feeling, and for months busied myself with the preparation of letters and critiques for publishing companies, discussions of which publishers would be sent the manuscript, and awaiting publishers' responses. Yet whenever I took a few quiet moments to reflect during these months, the feeling that my book was unfinished came to me again and again.

There is a part of my past that must be told, and until now, my lack of trust and total abandonment to the Blessed Mother prevented me from writing about it. She wanted something from me, and deep within, I knew what She wanted. If my story was to be told in its entirety, it must be completed with more courage than I had been able to muster until now. Deep inside I knew what part of my past still needed to be told, but I was afraid. I lost this fear when I found renewed strength in my Blessed Mother and through Her, Her Son. She would see to it that whatever the repercussions of my revelation would be, this revelation would be used for the greater glory of God.

What I did not possess until now was a total abandonment to and trust in God. I had agreed to trust the Blessed Mother — I had vowed to do that on October 7, 1991. Whatever was to happen was in Her hands.

On October 7, a warm Monday afternoon, I was consecrated to Jesus through Mary, according to the 33-day consecration described several hundred years ago by St. Louis DeMontfort. I had learned of this consecration through a friend who had been consecrated a few months earlier. I was in attendance with this friend at the Shrine of the Holy Name of Mary in Donora, Pennsylvania, where she and a small handful of men and other women made the consecration. The ceremony was officiated by Father Bernard. As I observed the ceremony, I knew that I was not in attendance by chance. Perhaps, I, too, was to entrust myself entirely to God in this way. A profound peace came over me as I shared this wish with my Blessed Mother. I had no idea what was involved in a consecration, or what was expected of me in preparation of making a consecration, but I was filled with confidence that if She wanted this of me, I would be given Her assistance.

I chose October 7th, the Feast of the Holy Rosary, as my day of consecration. Thirty-three days of preparation were required. In early September, I began the preparatory readings, as described by St Louis DeMontfort in his book, True Devotion to Mary. According to this treatise, preparation for consecration consists of personal introspection over a 33-day period of recommended prayers.

My wish for consecration on the Feast of the Holy Rosary was significant to me since it was through the rosary, the Blessed Mother's precious instrument, that I had been led back to Her Son. On the morning of my consecration, I reflected on what would be my new personal and individual responsibilities following a public commitment to a holier life. I felt an overwhelming sense of positive anticipation. Doubts about myself and my spiritual strength left as I entered the Shrine and made the consecration. My heart filled with a most quiet joy. I abandoned myself to my Blessed Mother and Her Son.

Following my consecration, a sense of release and relief filled my heart. I recognized again, but now in so clear a way, that, as I lay near death in 1986, God had intervened. He had returned to me my physical life and most importantly, my spiritual life, lost long ago. In the recent years of my conversion, I had become increasingly aware of Mary's intercession at that time and Her continued role in my life now. I am certain that without my Blessed Mother's patient love and tenderness, my conversion would not have taken place. At the time of my accident I had been so far removed from Her Son, that alone I could have never found my way back to him. On my behalf, My Blessed Mother interceded, and I now feel to some small degree capable and ready to live my life by God's Plan, whatever it may be.

I still struggle with questions about how I may best serve God and about the role I am to play on this earth. I will probably never understand. But I am now reassured by the knowledge that seeking to understand is contrary to faith; the desire to understand is a desire to control. Faith means no demands for resolute understanding or earthly control. Faith evokes complete trust and complete abandonment to a God whom we cannot see but who lives in the depths of our hearts.

My consecration allowed for a tangible representation of my surrender to God and a formal and firm commitment that, for the rest of my life, "God must first be served." If I falter in this, I trust that my beloved Mother will strengthen me, and in Her grace, I will continue, according to God's plan. It is through the grace of Mary that my fear in fully telling my story has dissipated; this fear has been replaced with the knowledge that revealing my very private secret may help other women, and men. What I write on the following pages is based upon my total trust in Her and in direct testimony to God's great love and mercy in my life.

A GREATER VISION

CHAPTER NINE

TOTAL ABANDONMENT ONE STEP FURTHER — FORGIVING MYSELF

IN THE FALL OF 1981, after two years of graduate studies, I received my Masters degree. It was a time of exhilaration, my studies were over and all possibilities lay ahead. I had sent professional inquiries throughout the Washington, D.C., area and across the United States. I decided not to wait in Washington for responses but to take a few weeks to travel. I traveled to Greece and Israel. I returned to Washington and to my temporary job as a waitress. Weeks of waiting for "true employment" had turned into months. Finally, in the summer of 1982, my "big break" came. A position had opened with the IBM World Trade Corporation in New York.

I also learned that I was pregnant.

Shock and horror set in when the doctor told me the news. She asked me if this were a happy occasion or a sad occasion. "How could this happen? It couldn't possibly be true," I told the doctor. But it was. The doctor asked, "What do you plan to do?" I slowly walked out of her office, my feet somehow placing themselves in front of each other. I was numbed and shocked. I found myself at my apartment, moving from room to room, straightening out small items in each room, sitting and staring, waiting for Tommy. As I sat, I gently placed my hand on my stomach. I felt disconnected with the reality of the event; I felt upset that something strange, foreign was growing within me, something that needed to be removed from my body and my life.

Tommy and I met that evening. He asked me what I intended to do. I did not answer. Instead, I asked him, "Are you ready to be a father?" His silence was my answer. I was not ready to be a mother, I told him. Not now—just when my big opportunity had come. I was scheduled to fly to New York in less than three weeks for the interview with IBM. The timing was all off, I convinced myself. A baby did not fit into my life right now, I told myself. Tommy did not protest.

The abortion was scheduled in early July.

I blocked out much of my memory of this day. I do remember sitting with Tommy in a large, brightly lit waiting room filled with other women and a few men. I did not bring my eyes to focus on anyone or anything. The only "self-programming" that I recall was not to catch anyone's eye. I could not have my eyes see their eyes because I was certain that my fear would be reflected back to me. The soft backing of the waiting room chair gently pressed against my back; Tommy held my hand; we hardly spoke.

I could control where I focused my eyesight, but I couldn't control the thoughts coming into my mind. I remember the hollow coldness I felt within as I tried to picture my parents' faces if by chance they would see me there—the rare kind of coldness that only comes when one tries to approach an idea or picture in the mind's eye so horrible and so incomprehensible as to be irretrievable even with the greatest of effort. I knew that my mother and father were ecstatic about my upcoming interview with IBM. How could I disappoint them? I was certain that I was doing the right thing.

The procedure went quickly. There was no physical pain, and as I lay on the table the only sound heard was a gentle sound of the suction instrument performing one of the most un-gentle acts of man. "This was my decision," I told myself, "I have the right to choose." A young black woman held my hand as I lay there. Her huge brown eyes looked down into mine. "It's OK," she repeated softly, over and over. "Was it?" I screamed inside. I remember asking God to forgive me for this act, and I could not dare to think that He might not. Within a few minutes a life was ended so that mine would not be inconvenienced.

Soon after the abortion I left Washington DC and Tommy. I was headed for New York and an international corporate life I could barely dream of. I boxed up my feelings about the abortion, labeled them as a regrettable choice that had to be made, and buried them in the back of my memory. I felt that I had accepted what I had done with responsibility and maturity, and it was time to forget and move on.

More than twelve years have passed, and I haven't forgotten. I don't believe a woman ever forgets. At times I found myself counting backwards...1983, my daughter — for I have always thought of her as a girl — would have been born; 1985, my daughter would have been a toddler; 1987, my daughter would have started grade school... My parents, with their huge capacity to love, would have adored my baby, held her, loved her, spoiled her to high heaven. I can especially picture my dad, beaming with pride, eyes shining with love, reaching down to scoop her up and just hold her.

Now, as I write, I think about the sadness this revelation will cause my family. They will cry, and they will be profoundly hurt. Yet one more time Joan will ask them to give more, and understand more, and endure more. But if, by my telling this part of my past, one young woman, or one young man, may be made to fully appreciate the enormity of the decision to cease a pregnancy and stop a life from being realized, then it will be worthwhile.

As I conclude this chapter I strain to find the words which may allow others to know that with time one inevitably reviews their past in different ways. Different things are revealed to people over time. My faith now tells me that no one has a right to take a life that only God can give. No one possesses a justifiable rationalization that overrides destroying a life. No one is assured that they will not feel at some point later in life the devastation of the act of abortion. I will carry the knowledge of my actions to my grave.

I have struggled to answer the question "How does a person come back from abortion?" In the years since my accident, I have learned that one must first accept God's forgiveness and grow daily in the awareness that God's love and mercy are always greater than our sins. This awareness comes only in prayer. Accepting God's forgiveness is a prelude to forgiving one's self.

Abortion is murder. One fewer person exists today because of something I chose to do twelve years ago. The reality of what I had done paralyzed me with fear and shame, though I would not admit that to myself for a long, long time. Even the protests to myself that it was a necessary choice because, "After all, it was my right, my body, my choice," — the argument I clung to for so many years — rang hollow in my heart. I realize, now, that in my soul I knew all along that what I had done was very, very wrong. But one grows comfortable with a lie after so many years. I did, to the point that I never even thought to confess what I had done to a priest. That is, not until my own conversion began through my introduction to Medjugorje. It was my Eternal Mother who brought me to the reality that I not only needed to seek out God's help, but God's forgiveness. And so, the lie had to end. The lie would be replaced by a peace I had not known in years. I moved through the steps of (1) asking for God's forgiveness, (2) accepting God's forgiveness, and (3) moving on each day in the awareness of God's forgiveness.

One cannot come to this awareness unless one truly comes to know Christ. One finds peace when one finds Christ, and one finds Christ in the Cross. This, I believe, is what Our Lady wanted me to understand when She inspired the words in my heart, "Love your Cross, daughter, for it has brought you closer to my Son and to Me." Peace would come only as I surrendered to the Cross of Christ.

It would be the Cross of Christ that would give new meaning to my life by causing me to reach out to God in a way I never would have without it. The way God changes a person is he permits them to suffer. My cross would break me from the evil that had held my soul in bondage all the years I chose not to recognize my sin, but to rationalize and justify what I had done. Satan lied to Adam and Eve by telling them that they could forget God, and by forgetting God, they could become God. I bought into this same lie when I chose to have an abortion. But God in his great love and mercy would not let the story end there. If I had been allowed to continue to live that lie, I would never have come to peace, for I would never have come to reconciliation with my God. In every abortion, there is a part of a woman that stops living. It is that part of her that seeks our her creator. And so, she goes on living in a body with a deadened soul. The life-giving force of God can only be resurrected in Christ. People can only come back to God through Christ. This is why God sent Christ into the world, to reconcile us with Himself. Jesus said, "I am the way, the truth, and the life; No one comes to the father but through me."

Christ is the Reconcilor.

If one truly knew Christ, abortion would never be considered a possibility. I believe that only conversion to a life-giving God will stop abortion and reveal the deceit so many have come to accept. Healing begins with awareness that abortion is sin. Sin needs more than forgiving, however; sin needs healing. And that healing cannot take place apart from Christ.

Jesus said, "The past is dead." My prayer has become "Please Lord, help me build a new future."

And he is.

There is great peace in my awareness, now, of having been reconciled, not only with my creator, but with the child I chose to abort so long ago. Though I denied her existence so that I could go on with my life, as I chose, I have come to embrace my child through what I have suffered. My child is a part of me, and I of her. That part of me is now with God.

Before I could receive God's forgiveness, I first had to acknowledge my sin of abortion, ask God for His forgiveness, and tell God that I was sorry. The sacrament of reconciliation was instrumental in my healing process, as God has always intended it to be. Only God could transform my most shameful act of abortion into an uplifting of my soul. It was God's love and mercy bestowed upon me through my suffering and through the patient, loving guidance of my Blessed Mother, that allowed me to be found again, and restored to value in God's eyes and in my own.

CHAPTER TEN

THANK YOU, MY LORD

MUCH PRAYER WENT INTO THIS WRITING, and particularly into this last chapter. I knew that I was quickly approaching this point in my writing when I completed Chapter Seven, "Medjugorje Revisited," in early June of 1989. For over a year this writing accompanied and aided the spiritual healing my soul had craved for years, and in the course of it, I learned that spiritual healing is paramount to all other healing, be it physical or emotional.

In late November of 1988, a month after my second trip to Medjugorje, I acknowledged that I would have to make more permanent arrangements for my condominium in New York state. It had stood empty, my belongings more or less as I had left them when I drove home for Thanksgiving nearly two years ago. Throughout this time I'd insisted on keeping it unrented, firm in the idea that I'd eventually return to my life and my work. Even as I accepted my new awareness of God's plan, my place in it, and the wonderful gifts the Blessed Mother had offered me, even as I regretted the willfulness and self-absorption that characterized that time of my life, a part of me still held to my old dreams.

Finally I decided to move my personal things home and lease the space to someone else. In early November, my father rented a U-Haul trailer and drove it to New York. My mother and I traveled by plane. He met us at the airport and drove us to Fishkill. Throughout this trip I felt stronger, more able to face the physical evidence of my old life, but actually packing it away was still very, very hard.

Inside my condo, the dust still reigned, and there was almost no sign that Mom and I had stopped there in February. Only when I touched the smooth case that held my rosary, and remembered how I had found it in my bedroom, could I imagine that the rooms had been untouched for two years.

As my parents packed up all my possessions — my paintings, the blue and lavender bedspread, the brass and iron bedstead itself — I sat listening and commenting, and thinking how my life had changed. That change had been painful beyond anything I had ever known, and the last bit of it still hurt steadily, but I regretted it less. That evening my mother and I slept on my fold-out couch. I could feel the emptiness around me, and I could hear my father breathing as he slept on the floor near us. I lay awake, confronting over and over the fact that this part of my life was truly over, and reminding myself again and again of what God had offered me, through His Mother, in place of it.

Spiritual journeys are long and difficult, and choosing to make one, as I felt I had finally consciously chosen in my last trip to Medjugorje, is only the first step. I had to make that choice over and over again, for my pride too often convinced me that I knew better what my life should be and what direction I should pursue. My spirituality grew slowly as I learned to see and accept God's Hand in every aspect of my life.

By early 1989, I attended Mass daily. My prayer life had increased, and I saw these things as manifestations of my spiritual life. I understood now how sorely lacking my relationship with the Creator had been. Again I recognized God's patience as He waited for me to acknowledge and ask for the assistance only He could give me. As my Mother Mary had worked to initiate spiritual change within me, She would continue to show me the way, to assist me, just as She has helped others throughout time.

As I look back on the years since the accident, I have learned to review all that has transpired in my life with eyes of faith. This has been God's great gift to me, be-stowed upon me by and through His Mother. My Blessed Mother would teach me to walk by faith, not by sight. No one, I realize now, could have done for me what She did for me — no doctor, no therapist, no friend, no family member could have helped me as She has helped me. My Blessed Mother has worked to free me from the guilt of my past, and the worry about my future. God knew well how angry I was with Him following my accident. I did not know how to approach Him sincerely and in humility to ask for what I wanted or, more importantly, what I needed. In His infinite wisdom and mercy, He sent me His Mother. I could approach Her, I wasn't angry with Her. I could ask Her for help without fear of the rejection I felt I might get from God. Amazed and humbled, I feared no reprisal from Her, even though I was all too well aware of my many years of neglect and ignorance. I found Her, not condemning, but more than willing to be used, as She was always used, as the doorway through which I might pass in order to become reacquainted and reunited with Her Son. She so gently but persistently has worked to keep me on the path God has chosen for me, a path of purifica-tion, a path of conversion.

Saint Paul wrote to the Romans: "We know that God makes all things work together for the good of those who have been called according to His decree. Those whom He foreknew He predestined to share the image of His Son, that the Son might be the first-born of many broth-ers. Those He predestined He likewise called, those He called He also justified, and those He justified, He in turn glorified" (Romans 8:28-31).

The Blessed Mother has played a vital and rejuvenat-ing role in my life since my accident, and Her presence with me is a great gift from God. Her presence in the world, when so many of Her children are miserable and also blind to their own spiritual loss, is a gift to us all. She is the Mother who chose to return to me, even though I had ignored Her for so many years. Just as my own earthly mother responded to my helplessness and need with love and care, my spiritual Mother gave me strength and faith, and showed me the path that led back to Her Son, back to reconciliation with God. I believe that She awakened me from the coma I lay in in 1986, but more importantly, She helped me awake from the spiritual coma that had stolen over my soul.

I attended Mass, received Communion, and prayed the Rosary daily; I went to confession monthly and fasted twice a week, in accordance with the directives She had given in Medjugorje. At first, I practiced all of this because I felt compelled to do so, because I believed the events in Medjugorje were the work of God.

These practices didn't take root in my life overnight; I fell short of my own expectations many times, but eventually I stopped condemning myself. Each time I failed at fasting, or found myself too busy to pray an entire Rosary one day, I accepted it and made a conscious effort to try harder the next day. I began to see the requests the Blessed Mother made at Medjugorje not as a series of demands, but as invitations from the Mother to Her children, meant to draw them closer to Her Son.

In effect, She presented me — and all people — with the means for growing into a more intimate relationship with Christ. Her call is a call to holiness, a plan by which we may come to see ourselves as the God-created instruments we were all meant to be, a way in which we can approach her Son again. The choice to follow the plan She offers is ours alone, for She is ever mindful, ever respectful of our free will. She does the inviting; it is up to us to respond.

I wanted to be an active worker in Her plan. When I returned from my first pilgrimage to Medjugorje in April of 1988, my spiritual healing, sparked by my experiences in that village, began. All pilgrims to Medjugorje are called to live out the Blessed Mother's messages in their lives daily, to be new disciples, carrying out the messages of Medjugorje through example, and to be active in our faith.

She calls each of us to put Her plan into action by living the Gospel messages of Christ. The messages given by Our Mother in Medjugorje are nothing new. They are the same messages She gave us at Lourdes, the same message She gave us at Fatima, and, the same message Christ taught during His short, three-year ministry on this earth.

Often when I speak I ask these questions: "Will we listen to Her call to us at Medjugorje?" Will we pay attention, this time?" Based upon our response to the calls She made at Lourdes and Fatima, our prospects don't seem great. But I refuse to believe that the world will entirely turn its back on Her call. She has said that Her apparitions in Medjugorje are Her last on earth, and that Her call is not, and will not, be heeded by all. While I could despair over these words, I have chosen instead to believe that She will stay as long as She continues to touch people's hearts, as long as She is able to prompt people to examine their lives. It was Our Lady who made me see the errors of my past, a past that contained a realm of serious sin and denial of God's role in my life. She helped me to see myself as God saw me, and the shame I felt prevented me from looking away. I had to come to terms with my past, but not live in it. And most importantly, I had to accept the great gift of forgiveness that God had granted me. With Her, as with Her Son, there was no need for explanation — only acceptance of my failures and of Their great love. Our Lady was gentle and patient, and exactly the instrument God knew I needed to prepare me for His work. What She has done for me is what She desires for all of Her children — that each one be reconciled with God. I believe, however, that if we continue to harden our hearts against Her, She will no longer come to be with us. When I look at the situation facing the believers in this world today, I can see that we have much work to do.

As part of this work, I have made a conscious decision to give witness to the events in Medjugorje, both through my example and through the use of the gifts God has bestowed upon me for this purpose. God gives each of us certain talents to use as we choose, but only He moves us to perfect them. If it is God's Will that I devote my life to spreading the message of Medjugorje through my writing and speaking, then I pray that I can be worthy of giving witness in a way that is pleasing to Him, and I embrace that mission wholeheartedly. For me, there can be no other way. Only God could have given me back my life, and I must spend that life doing what He asks of me. God left me to choose and pursue my own path in life for 29 years; I did only what I wanted, with little regard for what He might want for and from me. He graced me with many talents, and I used them to promote my own success in the world. In the world's eyes I was very successful, but in God's eyes I was lacking. Through my suffering, I have come to understand that we are not called to be successful, we are called to serve.

When my eyesight was whole, I made myself spiritually deaf to God's words, spiritually blind to the path He showed me again and again. In place of my eyesight, God has given me a greater vision, one with which I see myself through His eyes, eyes of love rather than condemnation. In order to gain this greater vision, to see myself as God saw me, to gain the true vision of my faith, I had to be stripped of everything I was, so that He might recreate me in the image He desired. Still, for many years I actually preferred spiritual blindness to the spiritual vision God offered me. With the Blessed Mother's help, I was given the grace to see this, offered a vision of the person I could be.

Only through my suffering, only through my trials, could God recreate me, refine me, remold me into what He wanted. I have come to realize that the way God changes people is through His permission of their suffering. Purification is painful, but as gold is refined in fire, so too would I be refined through my suffering, until I was deemed ready for His Hands, His service. I had to learn to accept my suffering as purification, and I had to learn to offer my suffering back to Him with praise and with thanksgiving. Suffering is God's redemptive love. The Blessed Mother told me to "love my cross" because She knew well how much I only wanted to be rid of it. Her Son did not reject His Cross, knowing it was through that suffering that God would be glorified. One must accept suffering before it can fulfill its purpose.

My physical blindness is God's gift to me, and my total acceptance of it will be my gift to Him. I trust that God will give me the grace I need to accept whatever crosses might come in the future. The question is no longer "if" I will choose to be the instrument He desires; it is only a matter of how I might best serve. Hundreds of years ago, my patron saint, Joan of Arc, explained her departure from the life she had always expected, that of a peasant woman who would be a farmer, a wife, a mother, with these words: "God must first be served."

Although I was not fully aware of it at the time, I made a decision to serve when I first sat down to write A Greater Vision. Through the events that drew me to Medjugorje and my experiences there, I realized that this world did not hold out for me all the things I thought I needed or wanted.

I remember sitting at the kitchen table in my parents' home on the morning of June 7, 1988, with a black magic marker in my hand, and a tablet of bold-lined "child's" writing paper in front of me, wondering where to start. "You should start at the beginning," I said to myself. Once I made that start, words seemed to flow directly out of my mind and onto the paper in front of me. Although I was often discouraged by the sheer struggle of writing the words down on sheet after sheet of lined paper, I never doubted the words themselves. I hurried to keep up with the thoughts forming in my mind, allowing words and sentences to spill out onto the paper with little thought of spelling or punctuation. The chapter titles, the sentences and their content — it was all there.

Sometimes I encountered dry periods, times when no words flowed, no thoughts but those of worry and hesitation filled me. The helplessness and vulnerability I felt as I reviewed those first few chapters came to me again and again. Those doubts about my endeavor and myself did not come from God. When these thoughts threatened to envelop me, to make me quit, I learned to call on God and Our Lady for help, and to trust in what I felt and heard from Them. God knew I was not a quitter, but He needed to make me aware of my dependency on Him.

Now that they are past, I can imagine these dry spells as grace periods, as well as trials; perhaps they were God's way of making me take time out, making me break away from my own unhealthy tendency to work continuously, unceasingly, until a job was completed. God reminded me constantly that He is the Conductor of all, and that we are only instruments to be played and directed as He so chooses.

I was filled with exhilaration when I came near the end of my writing, but I was also filled with loss and anxiety — a clear sign that I still had far to go on my journey in faith. The writing I had worked on so diligently for more than two years was almost completed, but where was my ending?

The ending I had dreamed of for months continued to elude me. No matter how I might try to deny it, the ending I had always envisioned for this writing was the restoration of my eyesight. "Please, Lord, don't fail me, now," I cried. "I need your help, as always."

Once again, God did not abandon me. He saw my fear, and my faith, which was not as strong as I professed it to be, and in His great mercy, He helped me once again.

In June of 1989, I returned to Medjugorje a third time, accompanying a group of a hundred people, most of them from the Pittsburgh area. Rita Klaus, whose story of physical healing was my initiation into the "Miracle of Medjugorje," went as well. "How appropriate," I thought, "that this woman, whose story introduced me to Medjugorje, should be on this particular pilgrimage."

For this trip, I had two thoughts clear in my mind. When I left Medjugorje in October of 1988, I had said a silent prayer to Jesus: "Lord, I promise You, if, one day, You find me worthy of restoring my eyesight, I will come back to Medjugorje and share my witness of Your love, power, and mercy in my life, in St. James Church, in thanks for all the graces You have bestowed upon me." I imagined that this third trip would be the one where my sight returned and the one where I found the ending for my book.

I cringe at the audaciousness of it. I marvel at God's patience with me, as He watched me try to orchestrate events to suit my own purposes yet again.

To say the least, the trip was not as I expected. It was as though God said to me, "Oh, yes, daughter, I will bring you back to Medjugorje and, yes, you will share your story with other pilgrims, but not inside St. James. You will give testimony to the wonders I have worked through you, and on you, outside, on the grounds of the church."

On Sunday, June 10, 1989, I stood behind St. James Church, sharing my testimony with roughly a hundred people. I smiled as I spoke, realizing once again that God had moved me to do His Will even as I had tried to impose mine upon Him. Somehow simply sharing my story with other pilgrims on such holy ground was enough. I was filled with a sense of exhilaration and peace, and I knew I was doing something pleasing for the One who had spared my life. I believe, too, that My Mother smiled down upon me that day.

On Wednesday our group climbed Mt. Krizevac, and we celebrated Mass at the foot of the Cross, where the Blessed Mother told the visionaries that She kneels each morning, begging Her Son to forgive the world for its sins against God. We stood upon this sacred ground as Mass was celebrated for all our intentions, all our needs.

That afternoon, our group went to see Father Jozo at St. Elijah's. From my previous experience, I knew that hearing Father Jozo would be a highlight of my trip. I also hoped that I might receive a blessing from him once again.

St. Elijah's was packed, but the crowd was quiet as Father Jozo spoke to us about his own initial disbelief of the apparitions and his acceptance that God was truly at work in the parish of St. James. He spoke of the Blessed Mother's message to us, creating an analogy which described us all as sources drawn to Medjugorje, the mouth of the huge river of peace and love that God poured out on us, and He told us that we were to be the rivers, the streams, the network that would carry Our Mother's message back to our homes, and far out into the world. None of us was in Medjugorje by chance, Father Jozo emphasized. Each of us had been invited there by Our Mother, and we had responded in a way that was pleasing to Her and to Her Son.

After his talk, I, along with another young woman from our group who had a special need, was taken back into his sacristy, and there he gave us his personal blessing. Everything happened so quickly; it didn't match the scene I had imagined as I planned this trip. Father Jozo laid his hands on the back of my head, just as he had done in April and again in October the year before, and he prayed fervently for several minutes. I stood motionless. This time, we didn't speak; I only thanked him, and we left.

On the bus ride back to Medjugorje, I kept reviewing my few minutes with Father Jozo in his sacristy. I wished that I had told him that my book was finished, except for the ending. He might have had some words for me that would inspire the conclusion I needed. But there had been no interpreter there in the sacristy with us, so I dismissed the idea, thinking, "It was not meant to be." In hindsight, I think this silence, this lack of reassurance about an ending for my book, was another test of my faith. I needed to trust that my ending would come, just as the title and all the chapters had come, with little thought or planning by me. I knew that I had to believe firmly that an ending would be provided, in God's time, not mine.

Thursday was our last day in Medjugorje, and I awoke saddened by that fact. The week, as always, had gone too quickly, but I took comfort in remembering the many blessings our group had received.

When I went to St. James that evening for the Rosary and Mass, I did something I had never done before: I sat near the front of the church, about seven rows from the altar. As we walked in, I followed the friends I was with. At one point, they ask me if I minded sitting that close to the altar. "Why not?" I wondered. On this last night, it seemed comforting to sit so close to the place where the bread and wine were consecrated.

When it was time for Communion and I approached the altar, I could tell that there were about thirty to forty priests present. Suddenly, one priest broke away from the others. He walked down the few steps from the altar, directly over to where I stood, held the Host in front of me, and said, "Joan, The Body of Christ."

I was startled and shaken; out of all the people crowded around me, why did he speak my name? How could he know it? Fleetingly I wondered if this was my sign. I said, "Amen," softly, then dissolved into tears.

"Who was he? How did he know my name?" My friends quietly asked me the same questions. I shook my head. After Mass ended, I walked outside, still shaken, and I heard a man's voice call out my name again.

"Joan — Joan, It's Father Don!" I turned around quickly, and looked into a smiling face and a pair of familiar eyes, the warmest and most tender eyes I thought I would ever see. I knew those eyes; I recognized the face. It was Father Don, the Jesuit priest I had met during my last pilgrimage, last October. We hugged one another, laughing and crying, and others stood about, watching our joyful reunion. At that time, I understood that the reunion not only with God, but also with each other is a great gift, one we long for constantly, albeit sometimes unconsciously. I knew my Mother watched from above, and I silently thanked Her.

My eyesight has not been restored. Although I still yearn for it, I do not mourn over these words, nor should the reader. My story is one of hope; hope means life has changed, not ended. I know now that my story was never meant to have an ending, only a new beginning.

A friend once told me "Your eyesight won't be restored until it doesn't matter anymore."

I looked at her incredulously. How could it not matter? How dare she say that to me!

But much later, as I meditated on her words, their truth was painfully apparent. God asks us to bear our sufferings and offer them to Him as a gift, but one cannot offer what one has never accepted. Mary's acceptance was complete, without reservation; mine must be too.

I still hope for the removal of my blindness. Even as far as I have come on my spiritual journey, I am still limiting God's role in my life. He asks that I fully accept my blindness, without reservation, that I bear my cross with love, as He bore His. Only my total acceptance will bring my healing, and the healing of my family as well, for my inability to accept has brought pain and division to all of us. My cross has touched my father, my mother and my sister as well.

Christ prayed in Gethsemane that God would "take this cup" from His lips, but He added, "thy will, not mine." One day, as I meditated on this mystery, I thought about my own trip to the Garden. In 1981, I actually knelt in the Garden of Gethsemane in Jerusalem, praying that God would help me find a job, and that He would take away the doubt about my career that plagued me. Unemployment seemed a great cross to bear at that point in my life, and God did respond, in His own time and in His own way. For a long, long time I begged God to take this cup away from me, to take away my blindness. Now I pray that I might glorify God by accepting His Will.

The lesson I have learned, am still learning, is not easy to relate. I lived in the "modern" world, a world in which every person controls their own destiny, in which suffering must in some way be the fault of the sufferer. While this was an exciting world, and one which had certain rewards, it was a flawed and incomplete world. Because my accident was not my fault — it was beyond my control — I saw my suffering as a great injustice. And yet, it is mine. If I was to survive my accident, my cross, I had to find a way to understand it, to accept it. The Joan who worked for IBM had no resources to allow her to accept her handicaps. If she had shaped her destiny, she had to take her injuries on as a personal failure, and their gravity would have destroyed her. I am not the same person at the end of this writing as the person described in its earlier pages. My suffering has changed me from a woman who had lived only for herself into a woman who made a conscious decision to start living for God. Through the grace of the Blessed Mother, I was shown that what I had valued before was not important. I am still alive, I still love, and I love more and better. I have been given more than I lost. I still do not have my eyesight, but I have learned that that can't stop me from doing what is important in this world, from loving and spreading a message of that love. Truly, I have a greater vision now, than any I have known before.

This is why my story does not have an ending, only a new beginning — a new beginning in Christ.

A GREATER VISION

There are approximately 4,000 abortions performed each day in the United States.

A GREATER VISION